AMERICA'S GREAT

AMERICA'S GREAT

GENE MOSS

Illustrations by
Clyde Olcott

ALPHAVENTURE

NEW YORK

Alphaventure
717 Fifth Avenue
New York, New York 10022

ISBN 0-915934-01-9
Library of Congress Catalog Number 75-18958

Printed in the United States of America by
Haagen Printing Co.

For C.J.,
who makes it all worth doing

CONTENTS

CONTENTS

CONTENTS

PREFACE

The very title of this book, it seems, is an open invitation to criticism. For who, indeed, is truly qualified to judge greatness in any human being?

This volume contains one hundred of two hundred sixty biographical sketches originally broadcast over the Mutual Radio Network in a series titled "Great Americans," sponsored by the International Brotherhood of Teamsters. Obviously, any program so named should include our country's Founding Fathers, as well as many of the men and women whose achievements fill the pages of our brief, but eventful history.

From the inception of this series, however, I have attempted to avoid the obvious. True, a good many of America's most famous people are to be found in these pages. Yet, rather than dwelling solely upon their more noteworthy exploits, I have endeavored to dramatize less familiar aspects of their lives, recounting their disasters and frustrations as well as their triumphs. In several instances I chose to profile some relatively obscure Americans whose contributions were, nevertheless, of considerable significance.

The result is a collection of stories of school dropouts who became brilliant scientists, penniless immigrants who founded mighty business empires, inventors who endured failure and ridicule before achieving success, a President who couldn't read or write until he was nineteen, and the man who invented the safety pin.

Included are a saint and quite a few sinners . . . an unlikely assortment, perhaps, but important

Americans all. There are, to be sure, some notable omissions, an unavoidable result of selecting a mere one hundred from a list of thousands who have left their marks on the pages of our nation's history. Many more will be covered in future volumes of *America's Great*.

FRANK E. FITZSIMMONS

The author and the publisher wish to express their deep appreciation to the International Brotherhood of Teamsters and to its general president, Frank E. Fitzsimmons, whose unfailing support made this project a reality.

ACKNOWLEDGMENTS

To Duane Kaye, who researched and drafted many of these sketches; to Tish Gainey, who edited this volume with diligence, honesty, and enthusiasm; and to Linda Moshontz, a remarkable typist under difficult circumstances.

To the dignity of man

He was a young man who had everything
. . . wealth, property, social standing, a
fine mind, and a strong, healthy body.
He grew up on his father's large, prosperous farm,
spending much of his time riding and hunting. He
was also a voracious reader and the possessor of
a keen intellect. He entered college at sixteen and
went on to earn a law degree. At the age of twenty-
two, he was elected to the state legislature and
soon became a popular and respected member of
that body.

Though he went on to a distinguished career as a statesman, his talents didn't end there. A witty conversationalist and a man skilled in social graces, he was also well versed in science and architecture. During his lifetime he developed several inventions, including the swivel chair and a plow designed with a principle still in use today. He never patented any of these, however, as he had invented them for the common good, not for personal profit.

Despite his wealth, his talent, and his aristocratic background, he was always a man of the people. He was one of the first to speak out against slavery, and it was he, more than any other man of his time, who fought for public education in America. While many in positions of power felt it was dangerous to educate the masses, he could not reconcile ignorance and illiteracy with the principles of democracy upon which this young nation had been founded.

What a legacy this tall scholar-statesman bequeathed to his country. Among his many accomplishments, he served as one of its greatest Presidents and fashioned the framework for public education. Yet, in his own epitaph, he chose to be remembered as a writer. For indeed, he had authored a document which was to become an everlasting monument to the dignity of man . . . the Declaration of Independence. Incredible as it may seem, he died just fifty years to the day after its adoption, on July 4, 1826. He was, of course, Thomas Jefferson.

Incident in Berlin

He was just a small, frail youngster when his father gave up sharecropping in Alabama and moved his family north to Cleveland, Ohio. As he grew, this lean youngster began to display a rare athletic talent. He could run, amazing his junior high school gym teacher with his blazing speed. As he grew older and stronger he became even faster and developed tremendous spring in his legs. While still in high school, he startled the track world by winning the senior men's AAU long jump championship.

He won a scholarship to Ohio State University, and in one meet at Ann Arbor, Michigan, he broke three world records and tied a fourth, all in the space of seventy-five minutes. The Olympic games were held the next year in Berlin. It was 1936, and the Nazis had started their ruthless quest to dominate the world. Their team had been training hard for this opportunity, as Adolph Hitler planned to use these international games to show the world that the Germans were, in his opinion, a genuine race of supermen. But one quiet, black athlete nearly destroyed Hitler's myth of Aryan supremacy all by himself.

He won the 100-meter and 200-meter races and anchored the victorious relay team for still another gold medal. But it was in the long jump that he applied the final, crushing blow. With Hitler watching, a German athlete broke the world record with a tremendous leap. The crowd roared, and the strutting little dictator announced he would personally congratulate the winner in his box. But on his final jump, the graceful young black American surpassed the German's mark by several inches. As the crowd sat stunned, Hitler angrily left the stadium.

More than a decade later the Harlem Globetrotters played in Berlin, and a huge crowd turned out to watch the famed basketball team in that same Olympic stadium. At half-time, a plane appeared and landed in full view of the crowd. As his arrival was announced, the smiling hero of the 1936 Olympics stepped out and waved. The standing ovation he received nearly rocked the stadium off its foundation, as the people of Berlin paid their belated tribute to the immortal Jesse Owens.

He refused a command

He came from a respected military family, and from the time he was a boy he dreamed of being a great soldier, yet he was nearly forty before he ever got a taste of battle. He had graduated second in his class from West Point, showing a superior aptitude for engineering, and when he received his commission he was immediately assigned to building fortifications.

He was still a lieutenant when he was presented with the difficult task of forcing the Mississippi River back into its proper course along the docks of St. Louis. Two sandy islands blocked the entrance to the docks. By building embankments along the Illinois shore, all the force of the river was brought against the lower island, washing it away and bringing the Mississippi back to the dockline. He was promoted to captain for that dazzling piece of engineering.

He was eventually assigned to a war zone, but even then it was to build military roads and bridges. Finally, he was given a combat command where his qualities of leadership and his tactical brilliance brought him a promotion to major. By the time war was over, he was a colonel, renowned not only for his ability and courage, but for the love and devotion he inspired in the men under his command. A few years later his career reached the ultimate heights, when he was offered command of the United States Army, the one promotion he was forced to refuse.

He had made his decision with a heavy heart and refused the position which, at one time, would have fulfilled his greatest dream. He still went on to compile a record of military leadership which earned him the lasting respect of friend and enemy alike. When the tides of war turned against him and he was forced to accept defeat, there were tears in the eyes of the victors, as well as the vanquished. Today military historians rank him among the most brilliant strategists of all time, though he achieved his fame in a losing cause.

His loyalty to the state of his birth had forced him to refuse President Lincoln's offer of command. Instead, he had chosen to lead the armies of the Confederacy during the Civil War. He was General Robert E. Lee.

They said it wouldn't work

He had intended to study for the ministry, but his father, a hardware merchant, was convinced his son had latent business ability. At seventeen he was sent to Philadelphia to apprentice in a hardware store, and after a few years he opened a store of his own. His generosity in extending credit, however, led him straight into bankruptcy. It was the beginning of a lifetime of indebtedness.

One day, while idly viewing a display of life preservers in a factory window, he became obsessed with an idea which was to change his life. The material employed in making those life preservers was in very limited use, because it was considered unstable. The young man, however, was fascinated. Surely there was a great future in that product; all it needed was the right man to perfect it.

With characteristic optimism and no knowledge of chemistry, he began a series of experiments. He melted the gummy substance on the kitchen stove and fashioned hundreds of shoes which he stored away in a shed. When the weather turned hot, his nose quickly told him that he had failed, as the odor of the melting shoes carried for miles. Undaunted, he continued his experiments, combining every ingredient he could think of to make the gum stabilize. But each time he thought he had found the answer, it turned into disappointment.

Then one day, as it happened with so many discoveries throughout history, a lucky accident occurred. While working with still another formula, some of the substance spilled on the hot stove. Instead of melting, it charred and hardened. Success, it seemed, was at last within his grasp.

After a lifetime devoted to an idea which had, indeed, become a mania, he had accidentally developed the process which would later be called "vulcanization." That single development led directly to the establishment of one of the world's great industrial giants, yet its inventor was never to realize a penny of profit. The man who helped to found the rubber industry in America was over two hundred thousand dollars in debt when he died. His name was Charles Goodyear.

Troubled genius

He was literally born on Broadway, the son of a famous actor of the day. For the first seven years of his life he trouped along with his parents, then was sent off to private school. He hated the school's rigid discipline, and though he was extremely bright, he was considered a "problem student."

After completing his prep school years, he entered Princeton, but his career there was a short one. As legend has it, he was expelled for throwing a beer bottle through the window of the college president.

He got a job with a mail-order firm, married, and tried to settle down, but he was too restless for that kind of life. His marriage ended in divorce and he began to drift around the world seeking adventure.

He spent much of the next couple of years drinking, gambling, and fighting in various waterfront saloons. Completely broke, he finally worked his way back to New York on a tramp steamer. Swallowing his pride, he asked his parents for money, but instead was given a small part in his father's play. For the next few months he toured with the acting company, an experience he did not enjoy.

The wild and dissipated existence he had led for so long caught up with him, and he was stricken with tuberculosis He spent six months in a sanitarium, and it was then that he began to think about his wasted life. He became a voracious reader of plays during that time, and upon his release, he embarked on his chosen career. He had decided to become a writer.

He enrolled in a class at Harvard to learn the technical points of drama, then began writing his own plays. His first effort was produced in a small Provincetown theatre which was a converted fishing shack; it was to be the beginning of one of the most illustrious careers in the American theatre. For during the next thirty years he wrote such powerful dramas as *The Hairy Ape, Desire Under the Elms, Mourning Becomes Electra, The Iceman Cometh, A Moon for the Misbegotten,* and many more. He won four Pulitzer Prizes and was the first American playwright to be awarded the coveted Nobel Prize for literature. When he died in 1953, no playwright had made a greater contribution to the American theatre than the strange and brilliant Eugene O'Neill.

It was in the stars

She was born and raised in Nantucket, Massachusetts, then the greatest whaling port in the world. Her father was a teacher, and from childhood she was fascinated with the work he did in assisting the seafaring men with the navigational instruments which helped them sail by the stars. She paid little attention to the existing prejudices about a woman's place being in the home. For she had a brilliant mathematical mind, and she taught herself astronomy not only by observing, but by reading works in French, German and Latin, as well as in English.

When she was fifteen she became assistant to the headmaster of a school and began conducting her own classes. The townspeople were shocked at the attitudes of this independent and strong-willed young lady, whose classes were open to all, while the other schools did not permit the children of black and Portuguese sailors to enter. As the years went by she developed a world-wide reputation for her knowledge of astronomy and was finally offered a teaching position at Vassar College. She was a remarkable teacher, sharing with her students the research which she continued to carry on in mathematics and science.

She didn't confine her activities to simply improving the minds of the young ladies she taught. Becoming aware that women on the faculty received less pay than their male counterparts, she threatened to lead her girls in a strike. The college board had no choice but to equalize salaries for both men and women.

She won another battle when she decided to apply for a class in higher mathematics at Harvard. Previously, the school had been able to reject women applicants because they didn't have the proper educational background. But she was an applicant with a reputation as one of the most brilliant scientists in the world, and again, the barriers came down.

During her distinguished career she won the Danish Royal Medal for a comet she discovered and was the first woman elected to the American Academy of Arts and Sciences. Moreover, she was the inspiration for many women to carve out careers of their own. Eventually, twenty-five of her former students became listed in *Who's Who In America*. She was our first woman astronomer, and her name was Maria Mitchell.

He believed in quality

He was born and raised in a small Massachusetts town, and his father had hopes of his son attending a fine university one day. But the boy was too impatient to get out into the competitive world of business, and so his formal schooling came to an end in the eighth grade. His first job was less than a steppingstone to success. He worked in a Boston drugstore, washing windows, scrubbing floors, and occasionally working behind the counter . . . all for five dollars a week.

At sixteen he went to work for his father, a rather successful cigar wholesaler, and settled down to what seemed like a comfortable future. But times were changing, cigarettes were just getting popular, and cigar smokers were becoming fewer. When his father died, he inherited a business which was in debt and struggling to survive. One day he called on a local drugstore and learned that the owner was anxious to sell his business. The store, which also sold candy, ice cream, and stationery, had debts of its own; yet he had been fascinated by this kind of business since childhood. In what seemed like a foolish venture, he sold out the cigar business and bought the drugstore, still heavily in debt.

As he had suspected, the store had suffered from poor management. The most neglected department seemed to be the soda fountain, where the previous owner had been using the cheapest products he could buy. But the young man had a totally different idea, and he developed a philosophy which enabled him to embark upon a career beyond his wildest dreams.

He began putting all of his energies, and a lot of borrowed capital, into developing his own high-quality fountain products. He experimented with his own syrups, purchased new and better equipment, and even bought a secret recipe from an old-world ice cream maker. That was the beginning of what was to become one of the most successful businesses of its kind in American history. The former cigar salesman built an empire which today stretches across the land and around the world. His name was Howard Johnson.

The courage to believe

ike the sons of so many wealthy and prominent men, he spent most of his early years as little more than a playboy. His father was a famous admiral, a lusty old sea-dog with an eye for the ladies, and a man who was known to European nobility and royalty as well. The son seemed bent on following in his father's footsteps, but despite his life of ease and comfort, there was another side to his character which was to keep him in trouble for much of his life.

He was, by nature, a fighter, not in the physical

sense, but for the rights of the individual against tyranny and injustice. This quirk in his personality came to the fore when he attended college. He was expelled, but not on the basis of his academic standing. While in school he had been attracted to a religious sect whose attitudes were opposed to many beliefs of orthodox religion.

Perhaps it was a reaction to the wastrel's life he had led for so long, but suddenly he was completely engrossed in his new-found faith, a religion which believed in equal opportunity for all people. Because of these views, the sect was persecuted, ridiculed, and discriminated against. Denied admission to meeting halls, he led protest prayer meetings in the streets, going to prison five times for his actions. He endured violence, threats, and abuse, yet he continued to fight for his beliefs. Finally, at the age of thirty-seven, he left his native country to settle in a new land.

He arrived in the wild, new land and took possession of some ten thousand acres which had been given to his father in payment of an old debt. He started his own colony, drawing up a frame of government which guaranteed freedom of worship and thought to everyone. While other settlers fought bitterly with the natives upon whose territory they were encroaching, his people lived in peace and harmony with the Indians near the settlement he laid out on the banks of the Delaware River. It was to become known as Philadelphia, largest city of the state founded by the courageous Quaker leader named William Penn.

So all might learn

He was born in abject poverty, and from the time he was nine years old, he had to work to help support his family. Yet he still managed to get an elementary education by attending school at night.

At the age of sixteen he traveled five hundred miles to attend college, working his way through as a waiter and a janitor. He was an outstanding student, and after graduation he was offered a job on the faculty. Meanwhile another school had been founded in a nearby state, and a principal was needed. He accepted the job eagerly, but when he arrived he found that the school hadn't even been built yet. Undaunted, he made arrangements to hold classes in a small church.

It was basically a trade school, specializing in teaching working skills to the handful of youngsters who comprised the first enrollment. No student was turned away for lack of money, and the students themselves helped to build the furniture for the struggling school's first permanent buildings. Gradually the surrounding community, impressed with the hard work and total dedication of the tiny school's founder, began to support it with donations from local merchants.

The years passed, and the little college grew, thanks to the tireless efforts of its president. He received support from the state legislature, and finally, national recognition. He was able to secure financial assistance from people like millionaire Andrew Carnegie and others. As his impossible dream became a reality, the obscure professor became one of the most honored and respected educators in America.

His task had been a difficult one. For he was black, and his college was founded in Alabama, only a few years after the Civil War. He knew, however, that the way up from slavery for his people rested in education. Today, Tuskegee Institute has an enrollment of over three thousand, and its alumni have made great contributions to America's growth in many different fields. Yet none could ever equal the achievements of the man who first opened the doors to learning for millions of black Americans. His name was Booker T. Washington.

He failed in school

As a small child in Germany, he worried his parents because he was so slow in learning to talk. In school he was considered a dull pupil, a boy with few friends who preferred to spend his time alone. He was good in mathematics, but had no gift for languages, and at the age of fifteen he was asked to leave school because of his indifference to study. He sought to continue his education in Switzerland, but failed his first college exams. He eventually was admitted to the Swiss Federal Polytechnic School, where he compiled a rather mediocre academic record, although he showed flashes of brilliance in math and science.

After graduation, he found and lost three teaching jobs before securing a position as an examiner in the Swiss patent office. The job wasn't difficult, and it left him time to continue his scientific studies. He devoted all of his energy to pursuing a theory which had engrossed his mind for several years, and, at the age of twenty-six, he submitted his findings to a physics journal. The publication of that paper was to have a staggering impact upon the scientific community. It attracted the attention of scholars all over the world, and he soon became internationally renowned. He was awarded the Nobel Prize for physics, yet, just a few years later, his work was attacked and ridiculed, and he was forced to leave the country.

He was perhaps the most respected scientist in the world when he was forced to flee Germany, the object of scorn and hatred because he was a Jew. So he came to the United States and became an American citizen, spending the rest of his life enriching the scientific knowledge of this nation. The kindly, eccentric genius, once a school dropout, made the nuclear age a reality by unlocking the deepest mysteries of the universe with his famous formula, "$E = mc^2$" . . . the equation for Dr. Albert Einstein's theory of relativity.

A *country gentleman*

He was the son of an upper-class Virginia landowner, and as a boy he lived an easy, gracious life. His formal education was sketchy, and though he was tutored in several subjects, he spent most of his days riding, swimming, and hunting. Like many families of the day, his was land-rich and money-poor, and the young man realized that he would have to find a career of his own.

He became a surveyor's assistant at sixteen and learned to rely on his own resources during long trips to wild, frontier territory. At the age of twenty-one he had his first taste of military action, when the lieutenant governor put the eager young man in charge of a mission to warn the French not to encroach on crown claims in the Ohio Valley. When war broke out he was commissioned as an officer and distinguished himself with his bravery under fire. He was rewarded with the rank of colonel, but after a bitter quarrel with his superiors, he resigned his commission.

He returned to military service when he was made aide-de-camp to a prominent general and was later put in command of all Virginia troops. By this time he had inherited land from his step-brother and had married a girl from a wealthy tobacco family. Once more he resigned from the army, able at last to enjoy the life of a gentleman farmer.

But as long smoldering grievances erupted into war, he was again called into action. They asked him to leave his life of comfort and lead an undisci-plined mob against one of the world's best-trained armies, knowing full well that he would be short of guns, ammunition, and supplies.

A lesser man might have refused, but he knew the very life of his country was at stake. Somehow he rallied his thousands of untrained recruits into an army, an army that fought courageously for five bloody years to earn one of the most glorious and improbable victories in history. On October 19, 1781, the British surrendered to the tall gentleman farmer from Virginia . . . General George Washing-ton.

He was once a writer

His father was a well-to-do importer, and the boy, who grew up in New York, had an easy and untroubled childhood. But all of this changed when he was eleven. His father was forced into bankruptcy, bringing about both physical and mental illness which culminated in a fatal stroke when the man was still in his forties.

The young boy tried to help his older brother support the family with small clerking jobs, and when he was eighteen he tried, and failed, at teaching. So he signed up as a cabin boy on an ocean-going ship. By the time he was twenty-five, the quiet, well-bred young man was living a life of freewheeling adventure. He jumped ship on his second voyage and shared the life of the South Sea natives, recounting years later that his tribal friends had been cannibals. He took part in a mutiny, lived the life of a beachcomber, and served a hitch as a regular sailor aboard a United States Navy ship.

Now he began to write about those experiences. His first books were well received, but when he wrote what he considered to be his masterpiece, he met with failure. The dark philosophies expressed in this new novel did not appeal to either the critics or the public, and his career as a writer began a steady descent into obscurity. He wrote more books, but he never again made a living from writing. Struggling with sickness and poverty, he finally found a job as inspector of customs for the Port of New York and remained at the post for over twenty years. When he died at seventy-one, the obituary in the newspaper noted that he had *once* been a popular author.

It was twenty-five years after his death that perhaps his most important work was rediscovered. That book, which he wrote when he was in his thirties, eventually became one of the great American novels of all time. It was the powerful sea drama of the search for a giant white whale called *Moby Dick*. It was written by Herman Melville.

Sure-shot

This legendary American, though identified forever with the Old West, was actually born in a small Ohio town, the sixth of eight children. This child had a special talent: an uncanny ability to shoot a muzzleloading rifle with more accuracy than anyone in the county. From the age of nine, the youngster was able to help provide for the family by bringing down quail and rabbit and selling them to hotels in nearby Cincinnati. Shooting matches were a popular pastime in those days, and like any back-country region, there were plenty of expert riflemen around; yet none could match this young child. Many a challenger came from other towns to test this shooting prodigy and left with both their reputations and their wallets badly deflated.

One day a professional swaggered into town offering to shoot against anyone for a side bet of one hundred dollars, and the tiny youngster won the match before a large and jubilant crowd. The professional was so impressed that he talked the young sharpshooter into teaming up with him, and before long they signed on with the famous Buffalo Bill's Wild West Show. They toured all over the country, thrilling crowds with such incredible feats of marksmanship as slicing the thin edge of a playing card held thirty paces away.

Then came a tour to Europe, where the show enjoyed even greater success, fascinating Continental audiences with such samples of genuine Americana as the famed Sioux chief, Sitting Bull. But the real hit of every performance was the astounding accuracy of the tiny star they called "Little Sure-Shot."

One of this beloved entertainer's most famous tricks was to shoot six holes in a playing card which had been tossed into the air. To this day, free tickets to sporting events, similarly punched full of holes, are called by that star's name. In 1946, a musical comedy based on this great performer's life became an all-time hit on Broadway. That show was *Annie Get Your Gun*, the story of the tiny girl whose married name was Mrs. Frank Butler, but who, during a career which spanned some twenty years, thrilled millions as the one and only Annie Oakley.

Not a drop was shed

It could have been a scene from a movie. The big, freewheeling adventurer is found in the local tavern, drinking, swearing, and brawling with a group of equally rowdy companions. The prim representatives of the government enter the saloon, hoping to interest the big guy in taking on an assignment which would be of enormous service to his country. It appeals to his desire for action, but there's also his outrageous sense of humor. He accepts the mission on condition that the government men try to drink him under the table. They lose the drinking contest, but America gains a hero.

The fiery soldier, whose intelligence matched his

self-confidence, put together his plan to take their objective. Few men would have dared to lead such an unruly pack of farmers, trappers, hunters, and woodsmen against a garrison of trained soldiers. And just to complicate the plot a bit more, an arrogant colonel from the regular army entered the scene and proclaimed himself in command of the expedition. After a heated argument, the big man agreed to compromise; the colonel could accompany him, if he kept quiet and out of the way.

Quietly they approached their objective, an enemy outpost. Overpowering the startled sentry, they poured in, whopping like savages, pounding down doors, and dragging out enemy soldiers. Their leader sprinted up the stairs to the officers' quarters, roaring and waving his sword, and was preparing to batter down the commander's door, when the captain stepped out, blustered for a second or two, then surrendered. The fort was taken, and not one drop of blood had been shed.

It didn't happen on a movie set. These were real men, a bit larger than life, perhaps, but as brave as any swashbucklers of the silver screen. The regular army officer who tried to cash in on the glory of that victory was later to become synonymous with treachery. His name was Benedict Arnold. The heroes of that famous Battle of Fort Ticonderoga were those rough-and-ready backwoodsmen who called themselves the Green Mountain Boys, led by one of the most romantic and controversial figures of the American Revolution . . . the legendary Ethan Allen.

He thought he lacked talent

He was born and raised in Salem, Massachusetts, and for most of his life his search for success was as futile as the infamous witch hunts which had once taken place in that same little town. He had a comfortable and dignified upbringing, studied with the finest private teachers, and entered a leading university. His college career was uneventful, though it did bring him into contact with many young men of influential families, several of whom went on to become quite famous.

He had decided to embark on a literary career, but his first efforts proved ponderous and dull. He wrote his first book right after graduating from college, then proceeded to destroy all but one story. Next, he wrote a novel of college life and paid to have it printed himself. Because it had failed to come up to the high standard he had set for himself, he bought up all the copies he could find and

burned them. For the next twelve years he continued to write and to read, devouring hundreds
of volumes in an effort to find a style of expression
for himself. During that time he often wondered
whether he really had any ability. By now many
of his college friends had become famous and successful, and he felt a sense of shame and humiliation at his failure.

He was becoming so depressed that his closest
friend was concerned that he would attempt sui-
cide. In an effort to restore his confidence, the
friend took a book of his short stories to a Boston
publisher, agreeing to reimburse the firm for any
losses they might suffer.

The publication of that book of short stories
brought him success and happiness. The book was
well received, and the author fell in love with and
married a talented young lady who had illustrated
one of his stories. Their marriage was a happy one,
and though he hadn't made a lot of money from his
writing, he had at least achieved some degree of
fame. Then, at the age of forty-five, he wrote the
novel which brought him world-wide recognition.
It was followed a year later by the book critics consider his masterpiece. The former college classmate of Henry Wadsworth Longfellow and President Franklin Pierce had, at last, attained fame on
his own. The man who had once burned his own
books was the superb artist who wrote such classic
American novels as *The Scarlet Letter* and *The
House of Seven Gables*. He was Nathaniel Haw-
thorne.

Partners in history

This is the story of two middle-class, Mid-western Americans whose lifelong busi-ness association eventually resulted in an achievement beyond their wildest expectations. For each of them, the inclination toward business began early.

When the younger boy was only eleven, he was earning money by making kites for his playmates, finding scrap metal for a junk dealer, and folding papers for a church publication. The older boy was even more inventive. At the age of fifteen he pro-duced his own wooden lathe, using marbles for ball bearings, and when the younger boy became interested in printing, he actually built a printing press for him. This was the start of what was to become a lifelong business partnership.

The boys decided to print their own little newspaper, which they named the *West Side News*, and before long they had over four hundred subscribers to their neighborhood publication. As they grew to manhood, the two partners, who seemed to share mutual interests in nearly every facet of their lives, decided to embark on another business venture. Both of them had always been very interested in machinery, and both were skilled and inventive craftsmen. They sold their publishing business and opened a shop selling, renting, and repairing bicycles. Before long they began to manufacture them, assembling them in a workroom above their shop. The bicycles they built became very popular, and as years went by, the business grew and prospered. When they began to turn their attention to still another field, something which had fascinated them since childhood, people began to wonder. This new preoccupation seemed so frivolous and illogical for two such down-to-earth business types.

The inspiration for the work, which was to consume the rest of their lives, was a toy they had shared as youngsters, a tiny paper glider which actually flew. On a cold December morning in 1903, their improbable dream took wing in a place called Kittyhawk, North Carolina. Yes, the lifelong partners were also brothers . . . Orville and Wilbur, the Wright Brothers.

No one did more

He was a native of Massachusetts and a member of a prominent family. He graduated with honors from Harvard and served his country well during the war. He had a brilliant career in politics, which culminated in his election to the Presidency of the United States. His lovely wife was a bright and charming asset, and his own intellect was acknowledged by all. There were some who worried that he suffered from a touch of vanity. Occasionally, his direct manner could turn to bluntness, yet he never opposed any public policy for purely personal reasons.

When he assumed the office of the President, the world was in a state of change. One power which had been an enemy in war was now making overtures of friendship. The President, following his own convictions, brought all of the prestige of his office to bear in creating a friendly relationship. This, however, angered the government of still another nation, one which had been a valuable ally during the war. Their government refused to receive the American envoy and suspended relations between themselves and the United States. Members of Congress were calling for an armed confrontation; the country was at a fever pitch. But the President did not call for a declaration of war. Taking firm action, he invoked American naval power in a show of strength. The world, which had been holding its collective breath, heaved a sigh of relief, as full-scale war was averted.

The Harvard graduate had taken bold action and averted war. Many may have disagreed with him, but there was no denying the strength and personal integrity he brought to the highest office in the land. Although his background and his handling of that crisis are reminiscent of a more recent President, let us refer to the ancient adage about history repeating itself. For the enemy which became a friend of the United States was England, and the ally with whom we nearly went to war was France. The year was 1800, and the man from Massachusetts was the second President of the United States, John Adams.

She was a princess

Her father was a man of great influence and power, yet when she was only twelve years old she courageously opposed his iron will. Feeling he had made a cruel and unjust decision, she interceded on behalf of those her father considered unlawful invaders and enemies of the people. He was so impressed by her fierce determination that he backed down and gave in to her wishes. She continued to help these strangers in a foreign land, bringing them food when they were on the verge of starvation. And once, when her father planned a surprise move against their leader, she took a desperate chance

35

and warned him, knowing that if she were discovered she might even be put to death.

It seemed as though her kindness had backfired when she was captured by another group of these invaders, who held her as hostage against attacks by her father's forces. But she was treated well by her captors, and during that time she met a young widower who fell in love with her. She agreed to marry him, and surprisingly, her father seemed pleased with the prospect, sending several members of her family to the wedding, laden with gifts. The marriage was hailed as an important one, for at last it seemed to insure peace between the foreign settlers and the ruling faction.

The young bride dreaded the inevitable visit to her husband's homeland, fearing she would not be accepted into his circle of society. To her great delight, she was greeted with open arms by her husband's family and friends. To make the visit even more pleasant, they were reunited with an old friend, someone who owed this lovely girl a debt of undying gratitude.

Ironically, she and her husband were not able to spend time with their old friend in England, because they moved in different circles. For he was a commoner, and she was considered royalty. Her name was Mrs. John Rolfe, and at the Court of St. James she was treated as a princess for, in truth, she was the daughter of a king. Her father was Chief Powhatan, the old friend was Captain John Smith, and she was perhaps the first American heroine. They called her Pocahontas.

All he could do was sell

e was born in Nova Scotia, grew up on a farm, and attended public school, although he never got further than the seventh grade. When he was eighteen, realizing that he had very little future as a farmer, he packed his bags and headed for Boston, where two of his older brothers were already living.

Big for his age and powerfully built, he got a job with the Boston elevated railway. After a year of collecting fares as a conductor, he longed for a chance to be a motorman. But when he tried to practice on his own, he wrecked a car and was fired.

Next he got a job as a gardener, but was soon fired again. Then he worked for one of his brothers who ran a delivery service, but he kept getting lost among the city's tangled streets. This time his own brother dismissed him.

Despite his obvious inability to hold a job, the big, smiling young man had a real knack for salesmanship. When a third brother came to Boston and started a small manufacturing business, he asked for a chance to go out and sell the product. He did remarkably well and saved enough money in a year to open his own business. He bought some simple machines to manufacture his product, using the basement of a married sister's home as a workshop. He made his products by night, then went out and sold them the next day. He wasn't making much, but for the first time he was in no danger of being fired. Gradually business began to improve, and he hired people to help him in his product's manufacture.

He advertised for sales help and received hundreds of responses. That was the beginning of a sales force now numbering in the thousands, the most successful organization of its kind in history. As the sales force grew, so did the number of quality items manufactured by the company which began in a basement and grew to be a multi-million dollar industry. It all began with a simple little brush, made and sold by a door-to-door salesman with a seventh-grade education. His name was Alfred Carl Fuller.

He wanted to farm

Though he was born in California, his widowed mother moved the family back to Massachusetts when he was eleven years old. The boy's life from that time forward was to be bound to the stony soil of New England.

He did extremely well in school, especially in literature, and at an early age he displayed a talent for writing. After high school he went on to Dartmouth College, but the academic life was not for him. He left school and took a job in a textile mill, devoting his spare time to reading.

At twenty he married his childhood sweetheart

and decided to resume his education. This time, he remained at Harvard for two years before giving up again. He became a country school teacher, editor of a small town newspaper, and finally, a farmer. That was the life he liked best, but though he worked hard on the land given to him by his grandfather, the farm was a total failure.

He took a teaching position at New Hampshire State College to help support his wife and four children. In his spare time he also indulged himself, as he put it, by writing poetry. Some of it was actually published, but with little success. Still not satisfied with his life, he packed up his family and moved to England, where he bought a small farm and continued his writing. Again he did poorly at farming, but as if by magic, his poetry became an instant success. A London publisher accepted his first book of poems, then a second, both of which received overwhelming acclaim. After twenty years of obscurity, he returned to America to find himself famous at last.

No doubt it was his lifetime preoccupation with the soil which gave his poems their special character. He wrote of simple things . . . an empty cottage, a grindstone, a forgotten woodpile. He had a way of making you feel the mood of a snow-laden New England forest, or the excitement of harvest time. And though he never fulfilled his life's ambition of becoming a successful farmer, he did manage to win four Pulitzer Prizes before his death in 1963 at the age of eighty-nine. His name was Robert Frost.

Lawyer and poet

He was born in Maryland and raised in comfortable circumstances. After graduating from college, he went on to law school, then opened his own office. He moved to Washington, D.C. when his uncle, a prominent attorney, offered him a partnership in the firm. He became a fairly successful lawyer on his own, but was never considered a brilliant one, probably because he was always overshadowed by his uncle and his brother-in-law, both of whom were among the most distinguished attorneys of the day.

No doubt one of the reasons for his failure to achieve greatness in the legal profession was his interest in other fields of endeavor. One was religion, and he confided to friends on several occasions his regret at not choosing the church as his life's work. Another secret love was poetry, something in which he had dabbled all of his life, though he never seemed to take his writing too seriously. Despite his comparative lack of success, he was pleasant and well liked, a handsome young man who always seemed to be in a hurry.

Immortality was thrust upon him in a curious way. War had broken out, and a friend of his, a prominent doctor, had been captured by the enemy. He agreed to negotiate for his friend's release, which meant spending a night aboard an enemy warship where the doctor was being held prisoner. He was successful in his mission, but of far greater importance was the poem he was inspired to write that night.

His poem, set to the music of a popular English drinking song, was published first in a Baltimore newspaper, then in several other periodicals. It soon gained wide popularity, as people all over America began singing the song written by the young lawyer aboard a British warship in Chesapeake Bay. The ship had bombarded Fort McHenry through the night, but in the morning he saw that the American flag was still flying proudly. That was September 14, 1814, the day Francis Scott Key wrote *The Star-Spangled Banner*.

She was born in Connecticut, long before women were supposed to be concerned with important matters, or to become known for their talents outside of cooking, sewing, and raising a family. Brought up in a solid, conservative New England atmosphere, she was somehow possessed of an inner spirit that would make her a crusader for justice all of her life.

The man she married became a professor at a small college in Maine, and it was there that she began to express a talent which would have a profound effect on the world in which she lived. She had discovered early in her life that she had a real knack for writing. She began to write short stories and sold a number of them, a welcome addition to the family's rather meager income.

Her thoughts began to dwell more and more on the most controversial issue of the day, moving her to begin putting her feelings on paper. She wrote three or four short stories which she sold to a small Washington, D.C. publication. The editor liked them so much that he asked for more, so she kept writing, still managing to keep up with her cooking and housework.

As she continued writing her stories, the thread of a novel began to unfold as if being woven into a great tapestry. Finally a publisher agreed to publish her stories in book form, and in the first year of publication, that book sold over three hundred thousand copies. Soon it was translated into dozens of foreign languages and was considered to be a significant factor in helping to plunge this nation into a war which threatened to tear it asunder.

They tell the story of her introduction to President Abraham Lincoln, who took her hand and said, "So this is the little woman who made the big war." Whether or not that incident actually occurred, the fact remains that the book, written by a New England housewife in protest against a cruel practice which she felt had no place in America, remains as one of the most important novels in our history. She was Harriet Beecher Stowe, author of the epic indictment of slavery, *Uncle Tom's Cabin*.

His work lives on

Born on the Spanish island of Majorca, this amiable, intelligent young man completed the equivalent of a college education and went on to earn his doctorate in theology. He taught and lectured for many years, but always had a desire to travel to some of the far away places he had read about. He finally fulfilled his dream when he was able to join an expedition to Mexico. They landed at Veracruz, and on the mountainous 260-mile journey to Mexico City, he was bitten on the leg by a scorpion. The bite became infected, and though he recovered, the leg was to cause him pain the rest of his life.

Spain had been in control of Mexico for over two centuries, yet little had been done in the way

45

of providing education for the tribes of Indians who inhabited the land. He learned several Indian dialects, and in turn, taught Spanish to the villagers as he traveled about central Mexico. More importantly, he began to teach them about farming: how to plant corn and wheat, olives and grapes. The Spaniards had sent sheep to this new land, and he taught the Indians how to tend them and how to weave cloth from the wool.

Word of this kindly teacher's work had spread, and the viceroy of Mexico asked him to accompany an expedition which hoped to settle the unexplored land to the north. That is when his real life's work began.

He kept a diary of the arduous three-month trip, as the expedition moved northward, over mountains and through vast deserts. But then they came to green and fertile valleys, and streams which ran down to a great ocean. This was the land which the Spanish had named California two hundred years before, and no man did more to make its golden promise come true.

Continuing his work of teaching the Indians to farm the land, he taught them many other things as well, including how to live in peace. He established a chain of beautiful missions which are still preserved today as historical monuments to his achievements. It is only fitting that a statue of this man now stands in Washington, D.C., selected by the people of California to represent the founding spirit of that state. He was Father Junípero Serra.

Genius equals prosperity

He was born in Missouri sometime during the Civil War. The exact date is obscure, because this now-famous American was born a slave. He was an extremely bright and curious boy, with a special fascination for the world of nature. He taught himself to read, and at thirteen he set out in search of an education.

Working his way as a cook and a laundryman, he attended one school after another, until he felt he was ready for college. His first application was accepted, but when he arrived in person he was turned down because he was black. Disappointed, but undaunted, he finally entered a small college in Iowa, intending to major in art. Soon his lifetime preoccupation with nature led him to the field of agriculture.

He was a brilliant student at the Iowa State College of Agriculture and Mechanical Arts and was offered a teaching position when he graduated. Two years later the great educator, Booker T. Washington, invited him to head the newly formed Department of Agriculture at Tuskegee Institute. He eagerly accepted and set about creating a working laboratory out of odds and ends he found about the campus of the tiny Alabama school. But even he never dreamed that the studies which took place in those simple surroundings would one day have a dramatic impact upon the economy of the entire South.

Faced with a sagging economy, the South, depending almost entirely on cotton for its income, looked desperately about for other crops to grow. It was this gentle black genius who showed them the way. Testifying before a congressional committee, he amazed the skeptical congressmen by showing them how 145 useful products could be made from the lowly peanut.

Ironically, the South was rescued from economic despair by a former slave; a man who became one of the most important scientists in the history of America. His name was Dr. George Washington Carver.

Brawler to hero

His father died a few weeks before he was born, in a Carolina log cabin, and the red-haired, freckle-faced boy grew up with a reckless spirit, a quick temper, and a remarkable faculty for getting into trouble. He grew wilder as he got older, and by the time he was seventeen, the tall, rawboned redhead was known as the toughest saloon fighter in the county. He inherited some money from his grandfather and went through it in one wild drinking and gambling spree. That's about the time he suddenly woke up and decided to try and do something with his life.

49

People just laughed when he said he was going to study law, but they failed to reckon with his fierce determination. He studied hard for the next few years and surprised them all by being admitted to the bar . . a bar of law, this time. The young lawyer headed west to Tennessee, where he soon made himself known and respected. He became a prosecutor, then was elected to the House of Representatives, and then to the Senate, all within a few years. Quite a spectacular rise for an ex-barroom brawler.

After a time he found political life boring, and he resigned from the Senate to become an officer in the Tennessee Militia. A superb horseman, he found the active military life much more to his liking. When war broke out, he demonstrated such personal bravery and ability to lead men in battle that he quickly became one of this country's greatest military heroes.

After the war he was again enticed into politics, and after another term as a senator, he became a candidate for the Presidency. But in one of the most vicious campaigns in history, his enemies sought to ruin him by spreading scandal about his beloved wife of thirty-seven years. She became seriously ill and died, her condition aggravated by shame and humiliation. So on the eve of his greatest victory, the tall, tough old soldier stood alone. They say no one ever entered the White House with a heavier heart than the man they called "Old Hickory" . . . Andrew Jackson, seventh President of the United States.

Birth of a tradition

At the age of five he arrived in America with his mother and sisters from Norway. His father was a carriage maker, an ambitious man who had come alone to America anxious to exhibit his works at the Chicago World's Fair. He then sent for his family, and the boy would always remember with pride his mother's calm courage in bringing them across the sea and halfway across the United States without being able to speak a word of English.

He had a typical middle-class upbringing in Chicago, learning to read, write, and speak English, and to play American games. He grew to be a tough, strong youngster, and a better than average student. He wanted to go on to college, but there was not enough money for that. So he went to work, planning to save a thousand dollars so that he could attend the University of Illinois. For a while he worked as a clerk, then took a civil service examination and became a mail dispatcher. He had struggled for four years to save enough money for his tuition, when two friends told him about another school which was less expensive. He took their advice, attended that college, and did so well that upon his graduation he was appointed as a chemistry instructor. Though he was to remain connected with that same university for more than twenty years, his ability in the classroom has been all but forgotten.

He had been a fine student in his undergraduate days, but he had also been captain of the football team. Along with his appointment as a chemistry professor had come the job of assistant football coach. Four years later he was made head coach. It was the beginning of one of the most extraordinary careers in American sports history.

He introduced new techniques to the game, emphasizing speed and execution instead of brute force. He became famous for his ability to raise his teams to an emotional pitch with his inspirational pep talks and was considered the outstanding coach in the game when his brilliant career ended in tragedy. On March 31, 1931, a plane crash took the life of the tough Norwegian who had made the "Fightlng Irish" of Notre Dame an American football legend. He was Knute Rockne.

The public forgave

His father was an actor of great talent who came to America from England, where he had established a reputation as one of the leading Shakespearean performers of the day. As boys, both he and his brother traveled with their illustrious father, and, quite naturally, both became actors as well. The older boy made his stage debut at fifteen and gradually began to establish a reputation as a fine actor on his own, though it took time to emerge from the shadow of his famous father. The young man's favorite role was that of Hamlet, and his brilliant portrayal of the melancholy Dane, precariously balanced on the edge of madness, became a standard against which future thespians would have to match their own performances.

He gained fame not only in America but in England as well, a high tribute to an American playing Shakespeare before critical British audiences. He toured the United States with his own repertory company, playing large cities and small towns where crowds greeted him with cheers at railroad stations and filled the theatres for every performance. When he opened his own theatre in New York with a production of *Romeo and Juliet,* opening-night tickets were scalped for as much as one hundred dollars each, a small fortune in those days. He gave one hundred consecutive performances of *Hamlet* in New York and was acknowledged as America's finest and most successful actor. Yet the pinnacle of his popularity came after a tragedy which threatened for a time to end his career in shame and disgrace.

He was well on his way to acting stardom at the age of thirty-two when his life was permanently scarred by a disaster which plunged the entire nation into despair and rage. His brother, not he, was involved; yet the scandal threatened to end his own career forever. An adoring public did not hold him to blame for the shocking incident, which, ironically, took place in a theatre. It happened on April 14, 1865, the day that President Abraham Lincoln was shot to death by the brother of the man who would go on to become the "Hamlet of all Hamlets" . . . the immortal Edwin Booth.

Champion of workers

B orn and raised in Boston, she graduated from college at twenty, then entered the teaching profession. Through her church she became involved in social work, something which her well-to-do family could not comprehend. But without her family's blessing or financial support, she still chose to follow the dictates of her heart.

She went to Chicago, where she worked with Jane Addams, whose famed Hull House provided both hope and opportunity to the disadvantaged. Inspired by her experience there she enrolled at the University of Pennsylvania for further studies, then went on to earn a master's degree at Columbia. She became an investigator for the Consumers League of New York, where her main goal was the improvement of working conditions for both female and child labor. Her tireless efforts helped to bring about new safety regulations and better working standards for all workers in the state.

Her work brought her to the attention of New York's governor, who appointed her to the state industrial commission. There she continued her crusade to protect workers, especially women, from unscrupulous practices of greedy and heartless employers. Though many challenged the labor codes which she formulated, the courts universally upheld the rulings which eventually brought about shorter hours, better safety standards, and more humane treatment for working people everywhere.

The distinguished career of this brilliant administrator became a milestone in the struggle for full citizenship for American women. In 1933 she was given the opportunity to fulfill responsibilities formerly entrusted only to men, when President Franklin D. Roosevelt appointed her, despite the outcries of many, to the highest position ever held by a woman in American government. She was named Secretary of Labor, a job which she performed with wisdom and integrity for twelve years, earning the respect of big business and organized labor alike. She was the first woman ever to hold a cabinet post in the United States Government, and her name was Frances L. Perkins.

An early retirement

ike so many famous Americans, he was
born poor. His father was a candle-
maker, and his early years were spent
working in the family shop. At the age of twelve
he was apprenticed to an older brother, who was
a printer. With little chance for formal schooling,
he educated himself by reading everything he
could get his hands on, including science, philosophy, the classics, even foreign languages. The brilliant youngster also had a talent for writing, and

he frequently made anonymous contributions to the newspaper printed in his brother's shop. Then, after an argument with his brother, he decided to strike out on his own. In another city he found a job as a printer, and before long he had gone into business for himself.

From that time on, one success followed another. He started his own newspaper, then a magazine, and while still in his twenties he had authored a best-selling book. His incredible mind kept him interested in a wide variety of subjects, and he was particularly fond of dabbling in science. He became a leader in civic affairs, and by the time he retired, a wealthy man at the age of forty-two, he was famous not only as a publisher, author, and philosopher, but as an inventor and scientist as well. Yet the career which would eventually bring him world-wide fame had not even begun.

His new career began with his appointment as postmaster general. Twenty-three years later, having become one of America's most articulate spokesmen against British tyranny, he was one of the signers of the Declaration of Independence. The remarkable self-taught scholar was also one of the framers of the Constitution, and in the years following the Revolution he became America's most respected statesman. After serving as our first ambassador to France, he retired for the second time at the age of eighty-two.

Scientist, inventor, diplomat, philosopher, and the most quoted man in America. The description could only fit Benjamin Franklin.

The peddler's idea

At eighteen the young Jewish clerk realized there was little future for him in his native Germany. Scraping up enough money for the passage, he made the long journey across the Atlantic to America, where his two older brothers had preceded him. He was disappointed to discover that his brothers were peddlers, not millionaires in New York. But with no skill or trade, and only a few words of English, he was forced to become a peddler as well. He learned quickly and soon began to earn a decent living. Although his brothers seemed content with their lives, he knew that America offered far greater potential. When he heard that gold had been discovered in California, he took his savings, bought all the merchandise he could, and sailed on a clipper ship around Cape Horn to San Francisco.

There was such a demand for goods of all kinds that he sold almost everything as soon as he arrived. He made a three hundred dollar profit, but now he had nothing left to sell except several rolls of light canvas with which he had intended to make tents for the miners. He bought a wagon for fifty dollars, loaded it with his rolls of material, and set out to sell it. But when one of the first miners he encountered told him of a special problem, he suddenly got an idea. It was then that one of the great merchandising success stories of America was born.

Nowhere in San Francisco could the miners find clothing which was strong enough to withstand the wear and tear of the rocky terrain where they prospected for gold. The enterprising young immigrant went to a tailor and had all of his material, a light canvas called "denim," made into pants in several sizes. He sold them all in one day, then set about improving his new product. Learning that the pockets often tore from the weight of heavy rocks and nuggets, he got the idea of fixing the pockets in place with copper rivets.

As the years went by, the pants he made became a staple throughout the West. He died a wealthy man, having founded a company which today is known all over the world. It all began with a few rolls of material in the back of a wagon owned by a little peddler named Levi Strauss.

And always, danger

He was born in a Chicago suburb, where his father was a doctor. In high school the husky, athletic youngster was a star tackle on the football team and also did some amateur boxing. Shortly after his graduation the United States was plunged into war in Europe. He tried to enlist but was turned down because of an eye injury he had suffered in the ring. Determined to become involved in the conflict, he volunteered as a Red Cross ambulance driver and was attached to the Italian Army. Wounded in action, he received two citations for distinguished service from the Italian Government. That was the beginning of his lifetime fascination with violence, war, and the imminence of death.

Twenty years later he was in Spain, observing and taking an active part in the revolution. In World War II, though he served in no official military capacity, the United States Government awarded him the Bronze Star for leading a band of guerilla fighters during the liberation of Paris.

In between wars he managed to keep excitement in his life by involving himself in such lusty and dangerous pursuits as bullfighting and big-game hunting in the wilds of Africa. By sharing all these experiences with millions, he became one of the most famous men in the entire world.

He was a writer by trade, and he wrote as he lived, with a powerful, forceful style devoid of tricks or flourish. Out of his World War I experiences came *A Farewell to Arms.* His adventures in Spain produced the classic novel *For Whom the Bell Tolls,* and his brilliant treatise titled *Death in the Afternoon* is still regarded as a masterpiece on the ancient art of bullfighting. In 1952 he received the Pulitzer Prize for his fascinating story of an epic struggle between a man and a great fish. It was *The Old Man and the Sea.* Two years later he was awarded the Nobel Prize for literature.

On July 2, 1963, when he knew he was dying of an incurable disease, the writer who seemed so preoccupied with man's inevitable rendezvous with death took his own life. It was a sad, but fittingly violent final chapter to the career of one of the most important writers of the twentieth century, Ernest Hemingway.

All her children

The frail young woman arrived in America with fifteen hundred other immigrants in steerage class. Though she was chronically ill herself, she nevertheless struggled through the miserable days of the voyage, tending her sick and already disillusioned countrymen. She had a dream of becoming a new American and of establishing a school and orphanage in the new land for other immigrant children. She also had a great fear of water, having almost drowned when she was a child. But before her life on earth was finished, she was to travel millions of miles across the seas, bringing hope to the poor of many nations.

She started with an orphanage across the Hudson River for the children who were cooped up in the slums of New York. Then she gave her energies to the Indians of the Southwest and helped to start orphanages and hospitals in the South for both blacks and whites. Mining families in Colorado needed her, and she went to them. She traveled to Seattle, Los Angeles, New Orleans and Chicago, planning hospitals and new homes for people from all lands who had immigrated to a place where they thought the streets were paved with gold, but found, instead, poverty as merciless as that in their homelands.

The press had become aware of her selfless achievements, and though a number of articles appeared praising her to the skies, she remained humble all of her life. Even when she was old and incurably ill, she continued to collect funds to buy land for what was to become still another school for orphans. She did not live to see it completed, but her work, and her inspiration, carried on just the same.

After becoming an American citizen in 1909, she spent her life helping others to find their place in this new and rapidly growing nation. Though she shunned praise for what she had done, she will never be forgotten. Twenty-nine years after her death the tiny nun was canonized, and in 1950, Pope Pius XII named her the Patron Saint of Immigrants. Her first name was Frances, but she was known to the world as Mother Cabrini.

Story of a soldier

This tall, well-built boy grew up with a fascination for soldiering, though he did not come from a military background. And though his family did not entirely approve, they did not interfere when he decided to enter Virginia Military Institute.

It was traditional to subject first-year cadets to considerable hazing, and during one of these sessions he was accidentally run through by a bayonet. He was nearly killed by the wound, yet he refused to give the superintendent the name of the boy who had caused the accident, knowing that it might mean an end to the young man's career. He recovered, regained his full strength, and became an outstanding student and a class leader. In his senior year he went out for football, and though he had no previous experience he became an all-conference tackle and captain of the VMI team.

After graduation, the young second lieutenant served first in the Philippines, then at several other army posts, where his intelligence and all-around competence brought him to the attention of his superiors. His administrative abilities brought him several promotions, and when World War I began he was instrumental in planning strategic troop movements and in coordinating several important offensives. His brilliance was noted by American Commanding General John J. Pershing, who appointed the tall officer as his aide-de-camp. In the 1930's, now a brigidier general, he was in charge of the infantry school at Fort Benning, Georgia, where he instructed many officers who would later become famous commanders themselves. He became one of this country's best-known generals, yet the accomplishments which the world will remember longer had little to do with his military career.

No one ever deserved the title of "soldier-statesman" more than this man, who served his country in many important capacities. It was he who suggested and helped to implement the program which enabled the nations of Europe to recover from the economic shock of war, and for his efforts he became the only career soldier ever to win the Nobel Peace Prize. Army Chief of Staff, Secretary of State, and author of the famed Marshall Plan, he was General of the Army George C. Marshall.

The life of the party

While others in his prominent Massachusetts family were becoming respected statesmen and national leaders, his life was filled with a series of misadventures. After graduating from Harvard he merely dabbled at the study of law, then wasted some more time trying to learn banking. Finally his prosperous father loaned him a large sum of money to go into business, but it trickled through his hands like water.

He received an appointment to a city job, but performed that task with such negligence that his department went deeply into debt, and he was faced with court action. He took over the family brewing business after his father died and quickly ran it right into the ground. At the age of forty-two he was penniless, and the sheriff was threatening to sell his house to pay off his creditors.

Undoubtedly one of the reasons for his repeated failures was his political activity, which caused him to neglect nearly everything else in his life. For he had become the leader of a radical brotherhood which included both working men and intellectuals, and he spent much of his time in bars and coffee houses, plotting political moves and inciting his followers with his bitter denunciation of the law and those who enforced it. Finally he decided on a bold course of action, the repercussions of which would be felt around the world.

The group of militants gathered at the appointed hour, and when their leader gave the signal they attacked, shouting like an avenging band of Indians. The date was December 16, 1773, and the place was Boston Harbor, where a courageous band of Americans dumped three hundred forty chests of tea into the water in protest against a tax they considered unfair. The man who organized that famous *tea party* was one of the real firebrands of the Revolution, a patriot who burned with the desire to see America gain independence from Great Britain. He was a cousin of the man who was to become our second President, and his name was Samuel Adams.

He'll never make it

Born on a farm near a small Massachusetts town, he received only a limited education. At the age of fifteen he obtained his father's permission to accept a job as a store clerk. But the extremely shy boy lasted only two weeks before his employer told his father, "That boy of yours means well, but he'll never learn to keep store in a thousand years."

At the age of seventeen he tried again, taking a job in a dry goods store where he remained for five years. During this time he began to keep a little notebook, in which he wrote bits of information passed on by salesmen and customers. Finally he decided it was time to seek his fortune in a big

city, so he headed west to Chicago, then a bustling
metropolis of eighty thousand people. There the
ambitious young man got a job as a clerk with a
wholesale firm and was soon promoted to traveling
salesman, covering his territory by train, horseback,
and sleigh. His quiet, honest manner quickly made
him a great success and he eventually became the
company's general manager. Then he borrowed
money to buy into another company, and within
ten years he had a full partnership in a booming
retail business. Fifteen years later he bought out
his two partners and began to operate the enterprise which would make his name famous around
the world.

Using many of the ideas he had jotted down in
his little notebook over the years, he introduced a
new era in retail merchandising. Prices were plain-
ly marked, and customers could exchange goods
if not satisfied. He made a special effort to attract
women by coining the slogan, "Give the lady what
she wants," and he was one of the first to create
attractive window displays. As the city of Chicago
became one of the world's great trade centers, his
name became synonymous with that growth, and
he showed his appreciation by becoming that city's
leading philanthropist.

The farm boy who failed in his first test as a
store clerk became one of the great merchant
princes of America, founder of a world-famous retail store and a fortune which spawned a mighty
publishing empire as well. His name was Marshall
Field.

A *political hack*

He came from a rather nondescript background, the son of a man who can best be described as a drifter. The boy received little formal education to equip him for any sort of future, though he was a hard-working youngster and earned much of his living at physical labor. He also did some farming, and at twenty-one he worked on a riverboat, then became a clerk in a store which went broke.

He served as a private in the army for a short while, then bought a partnership in a store on credit. The store failed within a few months, and it took him years to pay off the debts he had incurred. Then the likeable young man was hired as a surveyor, though he knew nothing about surveying. He learned well enough to get by and supplemented his income with odd jobs around town.

Still looking about for a better career, he debated between learning the blacksmith trade and studying law. He chose the latter and ran for the state legislature, but was defeated. Two years later, however, he ran again and won, continuing all the while to study law.

He became a good lawyer and prospered. But while serving four terms in the legislature, his political record was undistinguished. He voted the straight party line on nearly every issue and proposed no important legislation on his own.

When elected to a term in Congress, he continued on the same path to mediocrity, rarely taking a clear-cut stand on any national issues. His uninspired behavior infuriated his constituents, and in the next election they failed to return him to Congress.

He ran for office three more times, twice for senator and once for Vice President, and lost all three times. Suddenly, however, he seemed to be a different man, one who had awakened from his political apathy to become a powerful and articulate speaker on the burning issues of the day. Though he lost in his second try for the Senate, his ability as an orator had made the whole country aware of his brilliance. Two years later, the man who had once been called a political hack was elected to the highest office in the land. He went on to become one of the most important figures, not only in the history of our nation, but in the entire world. He was the sixteenth President of the United States, Abraham Lincoln.

He lived for adventure

His early life was not an easy one. His parents had separated before he was born, and his mother had remarried. When a series of misfortunes wrecked the family's finances, the boy was forced to work at an early age. He delivered papers, worked on an ice wagon, and set pins in a bowling alley, bringing every penny home to help support his parents.

From the time he had learned to read, he had been fond of books and had spent every spare minute he could in the public library. The stories he read, combined with his natural curiosity, had aroused in him a thirst for adventure which was to remain unquenched all of his life. When he was fifteen, he scraped enough money together to buy a small boat and began raiding the privately owned oyster beds in the bay near his Oakland, California home. For a while he was earning good money, but there were others in the same business. After one of many bloody battles with rival oyster pirates, his boat was destroyed.

At sixteen he went to sea aboard a schooner on a seal-hunting mission off the coast of Siberia. When he returned, he lived the life of a hobo, bumming his way around the country. At the age of nineteen he felt he needed an education, so he enrolled in high school for a short time, then took and passed a university entrance exam. He found himself too impatient for college, however, and soon he was off again, this time to the gold rush in Alaska's Klondike. When he returned home, he settled down at last to fulfill his real destiny.

He had always dreamed of becoming a writer, and now he set himself to the task. Drawing from his own experience, he wrote and submitted hundreds of stories, and his room was filled with rejected manuscripts before he finally began to sell a few. He was twenty-seven when the story which was to start him on his way to fame was printed in the *Saturday Evening Post*. This stirring tale of the frozen North was titled *The Call of the Wild*. It was followed by *White Fang, The Sea-Wolf* and many more adventure classics written by the one-time hobo, sailor, and pirate who became one of the most powerful storytellers the world has ever known. His name was Jack London.

He harnessed the falls

He was born in Germany and was afflicted from birth with a deformity which had been passed down in his family for generations. It seemed that such a frail child, humpbacked and with a twisted body, had little chance to amount to much in life. But there was nothing wrong with his mind. In fact, he was brilliant when it came to mathematics and could work problems with fractions before most children could read.

After an exceptional high school career, he entered college, where he continued to excel in such subjects as chemistry and mathematics. At first he devoted all of his time to his studies, including electrical engineering, a brand-new field at the time. Then he discovered politics and became active on the staff of the college newspaper. He wrote some articles critical of the government, but free speech was not permitted in Germany. He was forced to flee to Switzerland to keep from being arrested, and he realized now that the only place where he could find freedom and opportunity was in America.

He arrived here with little money and almost no knowledge of English. Through a friend he got a job with a New York manufacturing company. He immediately applied for American citizenship and learned to speak Enlgish quite well in a short time. When his company was bought by a larger one, his new employers were soon to learn that the most valuable asset they had acquired was the remarkable talent of this young man.

Within a few years he had established his brilliance in the field of electrical engineering. The company built a special laboratory for him, and his discoveries and experiments there helped it to grow into one of the great industrial giants of modern times. Among his countless achievements was his design of the dynamos and transformers which harnessed the mighty power of Niagara Falls. Though he became a world-renowned teacher and lecturer as well, he remained affiliated with that same company for the rest of his life. The company was General Electric. The genius was Dr. Charles Steinmetz.

A most regal lady

The little girl looked upon her grandmother's house as home, with its cavernous halls, the nursery on the second floor, and most of all, the attic, filled with strange and wonderful articles, where the child could escape to dream her dreams, away from the mischievous pranks of her two brothers. Her parents' occupation required them to spend most of the year traveling, so it was grandmother who ruled the household with a firm yet gentle hand.

The girl's days at convent school were happy and inspiring, for the sisters encouraged her in her love of music and instilled in her a sense of responsibility that was to affect her and her family to the end of their days.

She was planning a career as a concert pianist

when her mother became seriously ill, and the young girl accompanied her to California. When her mother died, it fell upon her frail shoulders to make all the funeral arrangements and accompany the casket back on the slow, sad journey to the East. She was only thirteen, but her childhood was over.

Her grandmother's business enterprise had ceased to make money, and she was forced to resume a career which, like the girl's father's, meant much traveling and little security. The girl laid aside her plans to go on the concert stage and joined her grandmother, entering the same occupation which her family had pursued for generations. It was the beginning of a love affair between her and the public which was to last for fifty years.

When her grandmother died, the beautiful young woman assumed the role of stabilizer in the family. Her youngest brother was only sixteen, but already handsome and wild, and she was constantly keeping him out of trouble. Her father had suffered a mental breakdown, and she worked to keep him in a private hospital. Even her older brother benefited from her selfless devotion, when she paid his expenses for two honeymoon years in Paris.

Yet her own career still flourished, and over the years she and her brothers formed a triumvirate unequaled in American history, as they became known as the royal family of the theatre. The princes were John and Lionel. The queen was the remarkably talented and lovely Miss Ethel Barrymore.

Heroic silversmith

His father had arrived in America from France at the age of ten, unable to speak a word of English. The family had arranged for him to become an apprentice to a leading Boston silversmith, and the young Frenchman, whose name was Apollos Rivoire, learned both the language and his trade very well. He became a journeyman, then a master silversmith, and was finally able to open a business of his own. He married and started a family, and before long his son had become an eager apprentice in the shop. The boy took over the business after his father died, and as the years went by there were three more young boys learning the silversmith's trade in the very shop founded by their grandfather. The cups, plates, shoe buckles, and other items of silver, gold, and copper made in their shop were considered to be the finest in all of Massachusetts.

By now the year was 1773, and trouble had been brewing in the colonies. England had levied taxes which the people believed to be unjust, and all over the land men of courage were rising up in protest. Though now almost forty, the prosperous silversmith took part in the famous Boston Tea Party, dressing as an Indian and helping to throw tea into the harbor. His biggest adventure was, however, yet to come.

It was two years after his participation in the Boston Tea Party that the master silversmith earned his lasting fame. As British troops marched toward Lexington and Concord, he mounted a swift horse and with little regard for his own safety, rode through the countryside to warn all within earshot of the coming attack.

He had been named after his father, Apollos Rivoire, but the name had been Americanized when he was born. It was the name made famous in an epic poem by Longfellow which told of his heroism on that fateful April night in 1775 . . . the poem that immortalized "the midnight ride of Paul Revere."

He danced for pennies

He was four years old when he and his family arrived in America, thankful for their escape from czarist Russia. His father was a rabbi, and the family settled in a tenement on New York's teeming Lower East Side. There were a lot of mouths to feed, and the small, thin youngster began working when he was only seven years old. His first job was selling newspapers on a street corner, earning just pennies a day. He also went to school and attended the synagogue, where his father trained him to sing the ancient chants of his people, hoping that the boy, who had a clear, sweet voice and an excellent ear for music, would become a cantor, or perhaps even a rabbi some day.

To his family's disappointment, he seemed to lose interest in both school and the synagogue as he grew older. He had found a way to earn money by singing and dancing on street corners, and the pennies and nickels with which people rewarded his efforts made him all the more determined to become an entertainer. At fourteen, he ran away from home and began to earn his food and lodging by singing current ballads in saloons along the Bowery.

He would hang around these saloons till closing time, and while the waiters were busy cleaning up for the next day's business, he would go to the piano and pick out simple tunes with one finger. He could only play in one key, but that was enough to launch him on a career which would make him world famous.

He began writing songs, and despite his lack of musicianship, he had a natural talent for pretty melodies and simple, yet charming lyrics. He sold his first tune in 1907, and four years later he wrote the song which catapulted him to fame. It was called *Alexander's Ragtime Band*. Within the next few years he had written the scores for half a dozen Broadway musicals and was the top-selling song writer in the country. There is hardly space here to list all of his great songs, but perhaps the one which will live on longer than all the rest is the little immigrant's tribute to the land he learned to love so well. The song is *God Bless America*. The composer is Irving Berlin.

They listened too late

He was born with nearly every advantage a young man could have. His grandfather was a famous railroad tycoon, and his father was a senator. The bright, handsome boy graduated from prep school and entered George Washington University, where he was captain and quarterback of the freshman football team.

When the United States went to war with Spain, the adventuresome youngster joined the army and was commissioned a second lieutenant in the Signal Corps. He served in Cuba, then was sent to the

Philippines, where he and his men braved jungles, swamps, and enemy fire to set up communication lines.

He decided to continue his military career and soon became interested in what was then a new field, aviation. He became an expert pilot, and when World War I began, he took command of an air unit in France. He became the first American to make reconnaissance flights over enemy lines. By 1918 he was a brigadier general, in charge of the largest concentration of fighting planes in history. Yet within a few years, his brilliant military career would end in disgrace.

After the war he became the leading exponent of air power, declaring that the security of our nation depended upon the growth of aviation, especially long-range bombers. But few military officials shared his beliefs, and as they continued to ignore his advice, his frustration grew. Always fearless and outspoken, he finally went too far in his criticism of his superiors. In a spectacular trial, he was court-martialed and found guilty of insubordination. Bitterly, he resigned his commission.

Less than six years after he died, his judgment was tragically vindicated when Japan's sudden air strikes dealt the United States a crippling blow at Pearl Harbor. World War II saw the emergence of air power as the most dominant factor in modern warfare, and ten years after his death, Congress paid a belated tribute to the man whose vision of the future made him a martyr to his cause. He was General Billy Mitchell.

He showed his gratitude

He had to work long hours on his father's farm when he was a boy, and he never acquired more than two years of formal schooling. He had an instinctive understanding of machinery, however, and was able to find work in the shops of Boston when he was sixteen. It was there that a casual remark by an employer gave him an idea which became an obsession. He was a good mechanic, but he devoted so much time and thought to his invention that he never held a job for very long. Soon his young wife was taking in sewing to provide food for the family.

After three years of failure, he finally developed a model that worked, but no one was interested in buying it. He found a manufacturer who would back him and pay him fifteen dollars a week if he would go to England to work on its production. He borrowed money for the passage and worked for eight months before he and his sponsor quarreled. Once again, he and his family were homeless and hungry.

He pawned his patent papers for money to send his family back to America, while he worked his way to New York as a cook on a steamer. Then fate dealt the last bitter hand, when he received news from Boston that his wife was dying.

Though he had perfected his invention, he discovered that during his years in England others had infringed on his rights and were actually in production. After a series of costly court battles, his competitors agreed to a settlement and invited him to join in a friendly alliance. After twenty years of poverty and frustration, he was suddenly showered with fame and money.

He never forgot his years of hardship and pain. The Civil War had begun, and though he was now a rich man, he enlisted as a private. When he discovered that the men in his company were disheartened and rebellious because their pay was long overdue, he quietly approached the paymaster and wrote a personal check for thirty one thousand dollars. That check was signed by Elias Howe . . . the man who invented the sewing machine.

He was the son of a man who taught him to think in terms of his responsibility to others. For a time the boy considered becoming a doctor, then a lawyer, but while he was at college, he turned to the one field in which he thought he could be of the most service to the most people. He worked at his books day and night to prove himself during those years in Pennsylvania. He was elected president of the student body and graduated first in his class. To prepare himself further, he earned his doctorate at Boston

University, then set out to put the principles he believed in into practice.

There was nothing impressive about his appearance. He was short and stocky, with no air of command. His voice was too soft, his manner too gentle to attract attention. Yet there seemed to be an aura of calm assurance about him, a quality of inner strength which impressed anyone who came to know him.

His rise to international prominence began because Mrs. Rosa Parks had been bending over a sewing machine all day, and her back hurt. When Mrs. Parks was ordered to give up her seat on a bus, she was just too weary to comply. So she was sent to jail for breaking the law of the city which said that passengers must obey the orders of the bus driver . . . black passengers, that is.

This was 1955, and after two hundred years of inequality, things were changing in the South. The black community was inflamed by the arrest of Mrs. Parks, and the city seemed ready to explode in racial violence. But bloodshed was averted by the efforts of the gentle, twenty-seven-year-old minister, who felt that firm, but passive resistance to injustice was the answer.

It is tragically ironic that his life was ended by the very things he preached against: violence and hate. Yet even an assassin's bullet could not end the work begun by this great man, whose dream of a better world will endure as long as people of good will inhabit the earth. That is the legacy of Dr. Martin Luther King.

A gift for his children

H e can honestly be described as an obscure American author, for though
countless millions are familiar with
something he wrote, very few people even know
his name. Born in Revolutionary times, he was
the son of an important clergyman of the day.
The boy was an extremely bright student and
entered Columbia College at the age of fifteen. He
graduated at nineteen, proficient in several languages and well versed in the classics.

He had originally intended to enter the ministry,
but he was never ordained. He was basically a
scholar, and eventually he became a college professor. He was also a prolific writer, though his

writing was confined mostly to rather ponderous
subjects with limited appeal. He also edited his
father's sermons, gave occasional lectures, and gen-
erally pursued the academic life. He was over thirty when he met the girl he wanted to marry, a
beautiful and talented young lady of only nineteen.
To the surprise of many, she married the rather
dull, studious professor, and they had six children.

There was, however, a hidden side to this man, a
delightful gift for poetry which he had never re-
vealed to the world. One night, when he felt particularly sentimental and moved by a special occa-
sion, he wrote a little poem for his children and
read it to them by the fireplace. He then put the
poem away and promptly forgot about it.

About a year later a young woman who was visiting their home happened to see a copy of the poem
he had written for his children. She asked permission to copy it, then sent it to the editor of a newspaper, who printed it. Copyright laws were very in-
formal in those days, and the poem was reprinted
many more times before the author's name was
ever made public.

He lived to be eighty-four, and though he published many works during his lifetime, the only one
he is really remembered for is a charming, little
poem he wrote for his children as he drove home-
ward through the snow one crisp and clear Christmas Eve. His name was Dr. Clement Clarke Moore,
and he called his poem *A Visit From St. Nicholas.*
It begins with the now-immortal line, "Twas the
night before Christmas."

Machinery was his life

The husky, keen-eyed young man was always fascinated by machinery. He was also stubborn, and after graduating from high school he refused to go to college, despite the wishes of his engineer father. Instead he took a job in the Chicago engine yards as a sweeper for ten cents an hour. By doing so, he could learn all about the huge machines which interested him. Before very long he had learned enough to become master mechanic of two entire divisions of the Chicago Great Western Railway.

He also had the knack of earning the respect of the men he worked with. Largely self-taught, he could work beside any man in the shop, then go up to the front office and explain in flawless technical terms just what was needed. The machinists liked him because he was one of them; the executives liked him because he got results.

He then turned his talents to a new industry and received one promotion after another. Within a few years he became president of a rapidly-growing corporation and was earning more money than most men make in a lifetime. But he had worked hard all his life, and confident that he had all the money he would ever need, he decided to retire at the age of forty-five.

A few months of idleness was all he could stand, and when one struggling company begged for his help, he was soon back at work. His family gave up hope of his retiring again when he announced he was buying the company, one which was in the comparatively new field of manufacturing automobiles. The main feature of his first car was a high-compression engine, something which only racing-car owners had been using. He modified it for use in a family car, and it became the sensation of the country in its first year of production.

Though he became a multimillionaire, he never lost touch with his old friends. The railroad workers and machinists he had worked with all his life were always welcome at the sumptuous home of the rugged ex-mechanic who founded one of the great automobile empires in American history. His name was Walter Chrysler.

His courage inspired a nation

Only the most desperate conditions could have caused the general to call this council of war. He needed a volunteer to infiltrate the enemy lines. It would have to be someone with military training, a man whose judgment could be trusted, and whose report would be accurate. There were several whom the general felt he could rely on, but when he outlined the mission, stressing the danger involved, only one young officer stepped forward.

His brother officers felt both admiration and deep concern for the personable captain. Many had known him at Yale, where he had been a superb athlete and a prominent member of the

93

literary society. After graduating he had pursued a career as a teacher, but when the war started, he had enlisted immediately, fighting with distinction in several battles. And though by now, his handsome face was scarred by explosion burns, his indomitable spirit was not.

Though several fellow officers tried to dissuade him from carrying out the mission, he quietly set about making plans. He would wear civilian clothes, disguising himself as a Dutch schoolteacher in search of work. And when he found the needed information, he would somehow have to get the intelligence back to headquarters on his own. He set off by boat on a Saturday evening, landed on the enemy shore at dawn, and vanished into the morning mist.

A week had gone by. The American army had retreated after the enemy had captured a major city, and there was no longer a need for him to continue risking his life. But before he could make his way back to the American lines, he was captured, interrogated briefly, then executed . . . without trial.

The hanging took place at what is now Third Avenue, between 66th and 68th Streets in New York City. There the courageous officer became a martyr to American independence, as he ended his brief speech on the gallows with the phrase which became a symbol of this young nation's struggle to be free. "I only regret that I have but one life to lose for my country" were the immortal last words of Captain Nathan Hale.

Hidden from the world

er home was in Amherst, Massachusetts, where she was raised in a strict, puritan atmosphere. A pretty and gentle girl, she attended the best schools and was very popular with her friends. When she was eighteen, she met a young man who was serving his apprenticeship in her father's law office. He introduced her to a whole new world of learning, like the poems of Emerson. These books served to open her mind, and she began writing poetry herself. When the young man moved to another town, the two kept up a correspondence, but he suddenly became ill and died of tuberculosis.

Shortly thereafter she visited Washington, D.C., where her father was serving in Congress. Still grieving over the loss of the friend who had meant so much to her, she met another man, the pastor of a Washington church who had become the most noted preacher in the city. His personality had a profound effect on the impressionable young girl, but he was a married man. Though they established an intellectual friendship which was to last for her lifetime, she never became emotionally interested in anyone else.

As the years went by, she became more and more of a recluse, spending her time in her garden or in her room, writing her verses of poetry. She became an almost elf-like creature, seen occasionally by guests in the house as a dim figure flitting like a ghost through the hallways. Finally, after many years, a friend prevailed upon her to submit some of her poems for publication. But before the world could ever discover her, she died.

Only three of her poems ever appeared in print during her lifetime. Today, more than seventeen hundred of her verses have been published, verses found neatly folded in the room where she had spent most of her fifty-six years. Perhaps it was meant to be, for surely she would have been frightened by the fame her beautiful poetry would have brought to her. She was Emily Dickinson.

A *matter of principle*

There were some who took an instant dislike to the brash, young West Point cadet. He was tall, handsome, and bright, and his father was a well-known officer in the United States Army. He radiated a self-assurance which came from having spent all of his nineteen years in and around one army post or another.

He made a few more cadets resent him when he announced his two major goals: to finish at the head of his class, and to one day become Army Chief of Staff. He proved to be a brilliant student and a good athlete as well, and before long his detractors began to realize that what seemed to be sheer conceit was merely a tremendous amount of self-confidence.

He quickly established another reputation, too, that of having the courage to stand by his convictions. In his second year, he missed some math exams because he had been in the hospital. When he returned he found his name posted on a bulletin board with several other students whose work was below par. Fiercely proud of his academic standing, he threatened to resign from the academy if his name was not removed from that list. The professor was adamant, and it seemed as though the young man's army career would come to an end over this simple matter of principle. Impressed by the young man's courage in the face of a decision which would have ruined him, the professor finally backed down.

The cadet went on to make good on the first of his ambitions, finishing his four years with an astounding ninety-eight grade average, highest in the class. Several years later he reached his second goal, becoming chief of staff of the United States Army. But these were minor accomplishments compared to his later exploits, as he became one of the great military leaders in American history. During World War II he was supreme commander of the Allied forces in the Pacific, and by the time he retired he had become one of the few men ever to earn the rank of five-star general. He was General Douglas A. MacArthur.

Ambition builds an empire

He was born on a small farm in central California. His father died when he was only seven. A few years later his mother remarried and they moved to San Francisco, where his stepfather was a commission produce broker. This was a business in which the boy, now twelve years old, took an immediate interest. He demonstrated his tremendous capacity for work by rising just after midnight each night to go down to the docks and inspect the arriving shipments of fruits and vegetables. The boy had a fantastic aptitude for gathering useful facts and figures, and the information he would relay to his stepfather enabled them to stay well ahead of their competition.

After school he would put in more time at work before going home to supper, homework, and then to bed at an early hour. The youngster was soon entrusted with both the buying and selling of produce, where he demonstrated a shrewd knowledge of supply and demand.

He passed up high school to devote full time to the business, in which he became a full partner at nineteen. The energetic young man, using a rented horse and buggy, traveled around and visited hundreds of growers and shippers, impressing upon them that any business sent his way would be handled with personal and painstaking attention. Within ten years his company, in which he now owned controlling interest, was the kingpin of the entire industry. A wealthy man, with no more worlds to conquer, he retired at the ripe old age of thirty-one.

Retirement didn't last very long. He accepted a position as director of a bank, but when his associates ignored many of his ideas, his competitive nature surfaced once again. "Then I'll start a bank of my own," he said, and proceeded to fulfill his vow. He opened his first bank in 1904, and trading upon his reputation among the many local Italian businessmen, he called it the Bank of Italy. Today, now called the Bank of America, it is the largest commercial bank in the entire world. Its founder, the ex-produce merchant who pioneered the field of branch banking, was named A. P. Giannini.

They called him a cowboy

He was frail and sickly as a child, but thanks to a gymnasium installed in their home by his well-to-do father, the boy grew up with a powerful physique. He attended Harvard, where he was a fine student. He married the daughter of a prominent family and entered politics. His keen mind and vigorous bearing made him a natural leader of men, and at twenty-three he was elected to the state assembly.

Then tragedy struck, when his young wife died after the birth of their daughter, and his mother passed away on the very same day. Shattered by his sorrow, he headed out West, bought a cattle ranch, and for the next several years lived the rugged life of a cowboy. Eventually he returned to the East, remarried, and entered political life once again. He became an energetic campaigner for his party and held several important political jobs, finally being named Assistant Secretary of the Navy.

When war broke out, he resigned his navy post to take command of a combat regiment. His reckless bravery under fire made him a military hero, and when he returned from war he ran for governor and was elected easily. Two years later he was nominated as Vice President, over the objections of many in his own party. For he was tough, honest, and outspoken, and some politicians considered his views to be radical.

A year later their fears were realized when the President was struck down by an assassin's bullet, and he succeeded to the White House. Moaned one political enemy, "Now that damned cowboy is President of the United States."

The man called a "damned cowboy" by one political enemy proved to be as energetic and courageous in the White House as he was in battle. Enraging his own party with many of his decisions, he followed his own conscience and is remembered for his crusade to regulate the power of big business, which earned him the nickname of "trustbuster." The outdoorsman, cowboy, conservationist, war hero, and one of the most important Presidents in American history was Theodore Roosevelt.

Talking leaves

This is the story of a remarkable Cherokee Indian born in Tennessee before the end of the eighteenth century. He fought under General Andrew Jackson in the War of 1812, and it was then that he first took notice of the white man's system of communicating by writing. He watched intently as they made their scratches with quill pens on sheets of paper, which the Indians called "talking leaves."

Possessed of natural artistic skills, he taught himself the silversmith's trade and became an expert craftsman. He also bought some paper and learned to draw pictures of animals and even portraits of people. The Cherokees had never developed a written language of their own, and he now began thinking about creating an alphabet for his people, a series of signs representing the syllables of the difficult Cherokee language.

When many of the Cherokees were driven off their lands, he became part of the exodus west to Oklahoma. There he continued to work on his alphabet, despite the opposition of the older chiefs. Finally his symbols were accepted by the tribal leaders, and the younger Cherokees, many of whom had already learned English, were now able to read and write in their native tongue as well. A special printing press was built for them, and soon the Indians were printing their own bilingual newspaper. He became a representative of the Cherokees in Washington, D.C., as thousands of Indians came to live in peace in the Oklahoma Territory.

English was the only language taught in schools by the time Oklahoma became a state, and there was no longer any reason to print a newspaper in Cherokee symbols. Yet this country will never forget the contributions of the Indian who helped to unify the entire Cherokee nation by teaching them to read and write. In tribute to his achievements, the tall stately trees found throughout the Western United States were named in his honor. They called him Sequoya.

And the job was done

It started in Germany, when a young man received his degree in civil engineering. But there was little opportunity for a young engineer in a country as reactionary as Germany was at the time. So he came to the United States and spent six long years laying out roads and sinking wells. Now he seemed further than ever from his goal of building the great structures he had envisioned for his new land.

He married, and a son was born, and he began to realize part of his dream by acquiring American citizenship. While working for the Pennsylvania

Railroad, he noticed that the canal workers transferred heavy equipment by means of hemp ropes, which frequently broke. It occurred to him that a great many problems could be solved if a rope of wire could be devised, so he invented a twisting machine which exceeded his fondest hopes. The invention, still in use today, made him financially secure. But he still had not created the engineering feat of his dreams.

His son studied engineering, enlisted in the army, and emerged as a colonel after the war. When he returned home, he found his father feverishly involved in plans for his most important structure. But one day, while the father was standing on a wharf, engrossed in his work, a ferryboat jammed against the pilings, crushing his foot. He was rushed to his son's home where the doctor had to amputate. Tetanus set in, and the great engineer died on July 22, 1869.

In spite of this tragedy, the construction went on, with the son taking his father's place. There were fires, accidents, lack of funds, and political difficulties. Workers died of a malady called caisson disease, a form of the bends. Finally the son collapsed from the disease, and at the age of thirty-five, became an invalid for the rest of his life. But from his sick bed, he directed completion of the structure his father had begun fourteen years earlier. It stands today as a beautiful, innovative monument to John Augustus Roebling and Washington Augustus Roebling . . . the father and son who built the Brooklyn Bridge.

She saved a few things

She was born in Virginia, and her upbringing was religious and rather strict.
The pretty and vivacious girl grew up
and married a young lawyer, but at twenty-five
she was widowed when her husband and infant son
died in an epidemic. A year later she was introduced to a rather prominent man, a highly intelligent and scholarly gentleman who, at forty-three,
considered himself a confirmed bachelor. He fell
in love with the lovely young widow, and despite
their differences in both age and religion, she was
attracted to him and accepted his proposal of
marriage.

Her husband was quite active in politics, and

107

she soon proved an asset to his career. She was an exceptional hostess, and her parties and social gatherings became the talk of the town. While others served punch and cake, her table was always beautifully and bountifully set, complete with an excellent selection of wines. She also possessed a remarkable memory for names and faces, enabling her to put a guest at ease with her warm and friendly conversation.

As her husband moved on to even greater fame and popularity, she earned the admiration and respect of all who came to know her. Then their lives were darkened by war which threatened to destroy everything about them. With the enemy only a few miles away, she was forced to flee her lovely home. At the risk of her life, however, she stubbornly refused to leave until certain cherished items had been carried to safety.

Her obstinate refusal to leave her home until she was sure that certain prized possessions were safe might sound like the whim of a spoiled and foolish woman. Nothing could be further from the truth. The things she insisted on saving were not personal possessions, but important and valuable documents of the United States Government, including a draft of the Declaration of Independence. The year was 1814, the enemy was the British, and her home was the executive mansion in Washington, D.C., where she and her husband lived and worked. He was the fourth President of the United States, and she was that gracious lady and fiery patriot named Dolley Madison.

His was the Golden Rule

His father was an unpaid minister who raised his family's food on a heavily mortgaged Missouri farm. From the time the boy was eight years old he worked to earn his own spending money. Once he set up a small watermelon stand outside the entrance to the county fair, until his father sternly reprimanded him for taking advantage of the sellers inside the fairgrounds. It was a lesson he took to heart, for in future years he was to acquire a reputation for fairness and honesty in all his business dealings.

When he was twenty he got a job as a salesclerk. Timid by nature, he did poorly at first, but gradually he gained confidence and became an excellent salesman. When he became ill, his doctor advised him to move to a healthier climate, so he went to Denver where he found a job working in a store. He did so well that the owner offered him the chance to open their new store in Wyoming, and to share in the profits. The ambitious young man seized the opportunity eagerly. His dedication to business and hard work paid off, and he was allowed to purchase a partnership in the company. Deeply affected by the generosity of his employer, he adopted those same principles. As the company expanded and opened new stores, he allowed each manager to purchase stock and share in the profits. There were over five hundred stores in the chain when the country was hit by depression. He poured millions of his own into the company, but finally, to meet his debts, he sold his shares. After thirty years of hard work and success, he was broke.

Close to physical and mental breakdown, he entered a sanatorium. When he had recovered his health, he went back to work with the organization he had founded, but for the first time, he now drew a salary. Within three years, he was off the payroll and on his way to rebuilding his fortune.

The man who became a multimillionaire twice in one lifetime remained active in business until he was ninety years old. He had called his original stores, founded in 1900, "The Golden Rule." We know them today by the name of the man who sought to bring that golden rule into the business world. He was J. C. Penney.

In defense of the damned

e was the son of the village eccentric in the tiny Ohio town where he grew up. His father was both an agnostic and a liberal, something which set the whole family apart from the rest of the community. On Saturday nights the townspeople would gather for one of their favorite forms of entertainment, a rousing debate followed by square dancing. The young man would always take the unpopular side in the debate, for he seemed to relish standing alone against the crowd.

He decided on the law as a profession, but he was an indifferent student and dropped out of the two colleges he attended. But he got a job in a Youngstown law office, and there he studied on his own, learning enough law to pass the bar. After a few undistinguished years as a country lawyer, he went to Chicago, where he became an attorney for a large railroad. After a couple of years, he resigned, having discovered that his background made him more in sympathy with the workers than with the corporation he was supposed to represent.

He left the field of labor law to become one of the country's best-known criminal attorneys in a very short time. He handled some of the biggest and most publicized cases in the country, often winning acquittal for his clients against what had seemed to be impossible odds.

In 1925 he became a participant in what was to become one of the most famous courtroom trials in all of history. He defended a schoolteacher who had been fired for teaching Darwin's theory of evolution in a Tennessee community where nearly everyone believed in the fundamental interpretation of the Bible. The whole world remembers how the prosecuting attorney, the renowned William Jennings Bryan, was humiliated by the country boy from Ohio who had dedicated his legal talents to the defense of controversial causes and people all of his life. They called him the "attorney for the damned." His name was Clarence Darrow.

Failure to greatness

He was born in a little Ohio town, where his father owned a leather tannery. He had no interest in the family business, but he had a real knack with horses. The short, stocky youngster was a better than average student, and his father was able to get him an appointment to the United States Military Academy.

Though he showed his natural ability as a horseman during his years at West Point, his academic record was mediocre. After graduation, the second lieutenant was assigned to a post near St. Louis, where he met and fell in love with the young sister of a former classmate. They were married, and for the next few years they settled down to the routine of army life. Then he was transferred to the Pacific Coast, but because the trip would be a hardship for his wife and their two small children, he went alone. The next two years were unhappy ones, despite the fact that he had been promoted to captain. Discouraged with military life, and longing to spend more time with his family, he resigned from the army.

The next six years were marked by one failure after another. Finally he accepted a job with his father's leather-goods company, but he showed no enthusiasm or ability for business. Nearly forty, the ex-army captain found himself with little hope of ever providing a decent living for his family. Yet within the next decade, he was to become one of the most famous and successful men in America.

War broke out, and men with military experience were urgently needed. At first he was used to train recruits, but was finally given a combat command. Suddenly, he began to reveal the qualities of a real military leader, as troops under his command scored one victory after another. He was promoted to colonel, then major general, and was finally rewarded for his efforts by being named supreme commander of all army forces.

When the war ended, he was a national hero, and on the strength of his popularity he launched his political career. In eight short years he went from poverty and failure to the highest office in the land. He was Ulysses S. Grant, commander of all Union troops in the Civil War, and eighteenth President of the United States.

An artist communicates

alf of his life was devoted to his career as an artist, yet few people know that this famous American ever painted a single picture. Born and raised in Massachusetts, he attended Yale, where he was an excellent student in all subjects, including math and science. He also had natural artistic ability, and after graduation he went to England to study under a prominent British painter.

He returned to Boston and opened his own studio, but had little success. People praised his work, but nobody bought his paintings. Nearly penniless, he began traveling through New England, offering to paint portraits for fifteen dollars each. His work was so well received that he was able to raise his prices, and soon he was painting as many as four portraits a week. Now financially well off, he returned home, married, and settled down to a comfortable life as a portrait painter.

He had never lost his interest in science, however, and his favorite diversion from his painting was attending scientific lectures. One of these lectures centered on the effect of electrical current in deflecting the needle of a compass, a subject which fascinated him. He had also read about some new signaling devices which had been invented in Europe. Suddenly he was obsessed with the idea of transmitting intelligence over great distances by electricity. While others laughed at his theory, he went to work.

His painting was nearly forgotten, as he spent the next ten years perfecting a device which could transmit intelligence through the use of electrical current. One day in 1844, a group of men in Washington watched in amazement, as over wires strung to Baltimore, some forty miles away, came the now-famous message, "What hath God wrought. It was written in a series of dots and dashes which was to become known as the Morse code, named after the obscure American painter who became world-famous as the inventor of the telegraph . . . Samuel F. B. Morse.

116

He ran away to fame

e was born to poor parents in Philadelphia, where his father made a living by
selling fruits and vegetables from a
horse-drawn cart. The boy attended school for
about four years, then dropped out to work with
his father. But the two quarreled constantly, and
shortly after his eleventh birthday, the boy ran
away from home. Now completely on his own, he
slept in the corner of a blacksmith shop and stole
food and clothing to survive.

For a while he worked in a poolroom, then got
a job delivering ice. By now he was living in an

attic for five dollars per month, and in his spare time he began to develop a skill. Practicing for hours every day, he taught himself to juggle, and for a boy of thirteen, he was pretty good. Soon he got up the courage to apply for a job at an amusement park, and to his surprise, he was hired. He had made up a little juggling act, and though most of the tricks were borrowed from other performers, it seemed to delight and amuse the audience.

Next he went to Atlantic City and got a job entertaining on the pier. He did so well that he was hired away by a competitor, and before long the young juggler was touring with a vaudeville company. He kept adding new touches to his act, including a very funny line of patter. His popularity rose steadily, and during the next few years he became a full-fledged vaudeville star, finally joining the famous *Ziegfield Follies*. By 1921 he was earning a thousand dollars a week, a fabulous sum in those days. Yet the career which was to make him much more famous had not even begun.

He starred in a Broadway play which became the hit of the theatrical season, and when a movie was made of the play, he also appeared in the film version. Within the next twenty years he was to make more than thirty films, becoming one of the great comedy stars of motion picture history. To millions, the ex-Philadelphia runaway, pool hustler, and vaudeville juggler was the funniest man who ever lived. He was born Claude William Dukenfield, but to the world he will always be the great W. C. Fields.

For all to see

He was one of the wealthiest men in America, yet he boldly risked his entire fortune when he stood up for what he believed to be a just and righteous cause. He was the son of a well-known clergyman. When he was seven years old his father died, leaving the family practically penniless. He was adopted by an uncle, a merchant of great wealth and influence, and went to live with his new family in their mansion on Boston's Beacon Hill.

He grew to be an intelligent and handsome young man, and after graduating from Harvard he entered his uncle's firm as a clerk. He made the most of his opportunity by working hard and learning well. After a few years, he was sent to

London as the firm's representative there. Upon his return he was made a partner in the company, whose business included importing, exporting, and the operation of several merchant ships. When his uncle died, he was left a large fortune and the responsibility of carrying on the business.

Under his leadership the firm grew even larger, and he became one of the most influential men in the country. Yet within a few years this rich, respectable gentleman was to become a fugitive from justice, an enemy of the government with a price on his head.

He really didn't have to become involved. He had enough money to weather any political storm and to stay above the battle which engulfed the rest of his countrymen, but that had never been his style. He threw his energies, his resources, and his courage into the fray, one time escaping through the woods to avoid capture by troops which had orders to arrest him.

When the rebellion became a war, the wealthy Bostonian left no doubt as to his participation. This famous patriot was president of the Continental Congress, the first governor of the Commonwealth of Massachusetts, and a framer of the Constitution. He is remembered best for the way he signed his name on one very important document. He said, "I write so that George III may read without his spectacles." Then he wrote what was to become America's most memorable autograph . . . the big, bold signature of John Hancock, on the Declaration of Independence.

From prison to fame

He was born and raised in North Carolina. He left school when he was fifteen, and after moving to Texas, he held a variety of jobs: working on a ranch, in a real estate office, and in a pharmacy. After he was married, he became a teller in a bank, where he was liked and trusted by everyone. Later, he ran a weekly newspaper in Austin and became a reporter for a Houston paper. Then, like a thunderbolt, came the startling news that he had been charged with embezzlement.

A deficit had been discovered in the bank where

he had worked, a shortage of $854. Unable to face the scandal of a trial, he left the United States and settled in Honduras, where he worked as a plantation bookkeeper, a druggist, and a printer. When his wife became ill, he returned home and gave himself up. His wife died a few months later, and it was nearly a year before he was tried. The evidence against him was not very strong, but he offered no defense, the fact that he had run away was enough to convict him.

For two years he worked as the prison drug clerk, from five each night until five in the morning. Then he became secretary to the prison steward, a position which allowed him considerable freedom of movement. After his release from prison, the humiliation of having been a convict was so strong that he never went back to his former life, or ever again used his real name.

While in prison he had written some stories and had sold a half dozen of them, earning about three hundred dollars. It was enough money to take him to New York when he was released, where he now dedicated himself to a career as a writer. He had developed his own, special style, a simple, straightforward way of telling a story which soon made him one of the most popular authors of his day.

Included in his prolific writings was one of the loveliest Christmas stores ever told, *The Gift of the Magi*. It was written by the ex-convict who was born William Sidney Porter, but who is remembered by millions as America's unsurpassed master of the short story, O. Henry.

Where hope lived

I t was her well-to-do Quaker father who first instilled a feeling for humanity in this frail little girl from Illinois. She would often accompany him on business trips to factory towns, where she was appalled at the wretched living conditions of the poor. She was a fine student throughout her school days, and after graduating from college she entered medical school. But her fragile health broke down, and she was sent to Europe to recuperate.

123

In Europe, especially in London's East End, she again was moved by the squalor and misery of the poor. She began to feel, that while she enjoyed the advantages of money and education, she was ignoring the suffering of those who had no opportunity to better themselves. She returned home determined to put her feelings into action. With the help of friends, she leased a huge house in one of Chicago's worst slum sections and set about painting, repairing, and furnishing the old mansion. She recruited qualified teachers and other volunteer workers to assist her; then opened the doors of the Midwest's first settlement house to everyone in need.

Soon they were instructing hundreds, most of them foreign-born, in such practical subjects as dressmaking and cooking, as well as music and art. Medical care and food were available to those who could afford neither, and children of working mothers were given supervision and warm meals. As news of her good work spread, others pitched in. One wealthy Chicagoan donated money to build a gymnasium, and soon nearby ramshackle buildings were torn down to make room for a playground.

The old house on Halsted Street still stands as a memorial to the great lady who gave help, and hope, to thousands during her lifetime. Four years before her death at the age of seventy-five, she was awarded the Nobel Peace Prize. It was a fitting tribute to the remarkable mistress of Chicago's Hull House, Jane Addams.

Movie hero

Born on a farm near a small Texas town, he was the son of a sharecropper who abandoned his family when the boy was still very young. The small, handsome youngster worked in the fields to help support his eight brothers and sisters. When his mother died, shortly before his eighteenth birthday, the family was split up, and the younger children were placed in an orphanage. The boy tried to enlist in the marines, but was turned down because he was underweight. Finally he passed the physical for the army, where, after a rather dismal start, he was able to rise from private to the rank of lieutenant in less than three years.

After his military career had ended, he made his way to Hollywood, having decided to try his luck at acting. He had no training or background for films, but his boyish good looks were a definite asset, and he began to get small acting roles. As he became a bit more polished and confident, he began to get bigger parts and finally some leading roles. Though he was never considered a truly fine actor, he did achieve considerable success in motion pictures, attaining the income and status which come with movie stardom. But gradually his popularity began to fade, and he found work hard to come by. He tried a series of business ventures, all of which failed, and after two decades in Hollywood, during which he had earned over two million dollars, he was forced to declare bankruptcy.

Although this story concerns the beginning and end of a relatively minor acting career, the actor himself will be remembered as long as American history is written, not for his Hollywood success, but for his exploits on the battlefield, where he won twenty-four decorations for bravery. The quiet, handsome Texan who had played hero in some forty motion pictures was the same fearless officer who, though wounded, had once single-handedly held off six tanks and more than two hundred German soldiers to win the Congressional Medal of Honor. In 1971 a plane crash wrote the sad ending to the life of the movie actor who had been America's most decorated hero of World War II. That was Audie Murphy.

Death wrote the last chapter

His parents were touring actors, who remained on the edge of poverty most of the time. His father, a heavy drinker, finally abandoned his wife and three children. Shortly thereafter, the young wife died, and the children were taken in by family friends.

This moody and sensitive boy was adopted by a wealthy tobacco merchant and his wife. His foster parents were very strict, and he was glad to be sent to a private school in England. When he returned, he entered a military academy, then went on to a university attended by many young men of well-to-do families. But his frugal stepfather supplied him with little spending money, so he began to gamble for a living. Then, when a girl he had been romancing married someone else, the bitter young man left college. After a short stint in the army, his foster father reluctantly helped him secure an appointment to West Point. The rigid discipline of the academy, however, was not for him, and after many breaches of the rules, he was expelled.

Having given up on a military career, he turned to another field in which he had displayed some talent during his school days. He began to write, first poetry, then fiction, and when one of his short stories won a fifty dollar prize, he was encouraged to go on. He got a job as an editor of a literary magazine, married, and seemed headed, at last, for a happy and successful future.

He was literary editor of a prominent magazine when tragedy struck without warning. His lovely young wife suffered a stroke, and after lingering for another four years, she died. It was a blow from which he never recovered. His worry over his wife had driven him to drink, and after her death he seemed to sink into a bottomless pit of despair. He continued to write brilliantly, though his work reflected the sense of horror and sadness which had infected his entire being. He died an alcoholic on a Baltimore street, the last tragic ending for one of the truly great writers of American history . . . the author of *The Raven, The Murders in the Rue Morgue,* and *Annabel Lee,* just a few of many mournful masterpieces created by the genius of Edgar Allan Poe.

A way to help his country

The young Jew had seen his share of persecution and war in his native Poland. Forced to flee, and separated from his family, he passed through many European countries, learning several languages and acquiring business and banking skills as well. At last he found a country where he could live in peace and freedom, and he became a successful broker and commission merchant. He married and settled down to build a life for himself and his family.

When his new country was plunged into war, he could not stand idly by. Though he was neither young nor healthy enough to become a soldier, he joined an underground organization, where his knowledge of languages made him invaluable. His fluent German allowed him to infiltrate enemy troops, but eventually his espionage was discovered, and he was arrested and sentenced to die. But with the help of friends in the underground, he effected his escape. By the time he finally made his way back home, his health was completely shattered. Yet he still felt there was something more he could do to help his country's cause.

His new weapon became money, for funds were desperately needed for guns, ammunition, and supplies. He had built a sizeable fortune of his own and had become a highly respected and powerful force in the world of commerce. Working in co-operation with the country's leading banker, he used his influence to obtain loans which helped to finance the war. He also used most of his personal fortune to aid in the fight, and when victory was finally won he was practically penniless.

The army he helped to feed and clothe was the Continental army, under the command of George Washington. The German troops he had infiltrated as a spy were the paid Hessians, serving under the British. Before he died, in 1785, he had seen his beloved country, the United States of America, gain freedom from the opression he had learned to despise in the ghettos of Europe. His name was Haym Salomon.

So others might speak

This is the story of a man who devoted most of his life to something other than what the world remembers him for. He was born in Edinburgh, Scotland, where his father, like his father before him, was a teacher of speech. So it was quite natural for the boy to become interested in the subject.

He decided, at an early age, to follow in his father's footsteps. He went to high school, then went to London where his grandfather was still teaching elocution. The old gentleman's library was filled with books on speech and acoustics, and the boy read them eagerly, learning more in that year than all of his previous training had taught

131

him. After that he attended the University of Edinburgh, still pursuing the science of sound.

When his father was invited to America for a series of lectures, the young man came along. He accepted a teaching position at a Boston school for the deaf, where he was now able to put all of his knowledge into practice. His methods produced remarkable results, and he now knew that the teaching of the deaf would be his real mission in life. He opened his own school of vocal physiology and soon was teaching children of some of Boston's wealthiest families, including one lovely girl who later became his wife.

In his spare time he continued to study and experiment with the science of sound. He had been using a device which electrically created sound vibrations detectable by the human ear. Suddenly he had an idea, an idea so exciting that it was to consume nearly all of his time for the next three years.

Setting aside his teaching, he now devoted all of his efforts to his new experiments with electric sound transmission. Aided by financial backing and a hard-working assistant, he was finally ready to test the new device, a battery-operated machine which he claimed could transmit the human voice. His first message wasn't very dramatic, as out of the crude apparatus came the words, "Mr. Watson, come here, I want you." The date was March 10, 1876. The twenty-nine-year-old teacher of the deaf, Alexander Graham Bell, had invented the telephone.

Against unseen dangers

She was born in a small Pennsylvania town and grew up in a typical suburban atmosphere. But her mother taught her an appreciation of nature, and as a child she learned to love the birds, insects, and plant life which could be found in the surrounding countryside. This preoccupation with nature was to have a profound and lasting effect upon her life.

After graduation from high school she entered college with the intent of becoming a writer. But a course in life science renewed her interest in nature, and she switched her major, graduating with a degree in biology. Now determined to pursue a career as a scientist, she went on to earn a master's degree, then began teaching. The quiet, gentle biologist spent fifteen years working in the laboratories of the United States Fish and Wildlife Service, writing and editing various government publications; it was a life of relative obscurity. Yet this shy and brilliant lady was to become the center of controversy, as she almost single-handedly awakened the world to dangers which few of us ever dreamed existed.

She had begun to write, displaying not only her great knowledge of science, but a clear and fascinating literary style as well. She wrote of what she knew and loved, the world of nature. Soon her eloquent books, backed by scientific facts, began to bring her fame, but her most important contribution still lay ahead.

She had written of the sea, fascinating millions of readers as she described life beneath the great oceans. But now there was another book which had to be written. It took her four years to complete, as she wrote and rewrote her manuscript, putting her scientific data into straightforward language which all people could understand. In the middle of this great project, she learned she had cancer, providing even more impetus to her completing the book before it was too late. That book aroused the entire world to the dangers of chemical pollution and helped to usher in the age of ecology. It was called *Silent Spring,* and its author, who died before she received the credit she so richly deserved, was Rachel Carson.

He learned to read and write

He came from the most humble of beginnings. His father died when he was only three, and his mother was forced to take in washing and sewing to support the family. At ten the boy was apprenticed to a tailor, a strict and harsh master. At sixteen he ran away, settling in another state where he managed to open a small tailor shop of his own. His life took a turn for the better when he met the girl who was to become his wife. The young couple lived in the back of the tailor shop, and the lovely, well-educated girl taught her husband to read . . . at the age of nineteen!

Though he had little education, she had perceived that he had a fine mind. In addition to studying with his wife, he attended lectures and debates at a nearby college, thirstily absorbing all the knowledge he could. He soon began to engage in public debates himself, and before long his intelligence and his honest, forthright manner began to attract attention. By the time he was twenty-one he was popular enough to be elected alderman, and within a year he was mayor of the town.

Ruggedly handsome, and a compelling speaker, he went on to state politics, becoming a legislator, a governor, a congressman, then a United States senator. Yet he always remembered his lowly origins and never lost his distrust of those with wealth and polish, traits which often grated on the nerves of his colleagues and made him some enemies along the way.

His selection as a vice-presidential candidate came as a surprise to many in both parties. And when, in the wake of one of this nation's greatest tragedies, he became President, he found himself in the center of a political storm. For he was a Southerner who had put the Union ahead of regional prejudices, and now his enemies descended like wolves. He was the only President to be impeached and tried, yet the vote failed to remove him from office. History has shown, however, that Abraham Lincoln had chosen a man of great integrity and courage when he selected the tailor from Tennessee as his running mate. He was Andrew Johnson, seventeenth President of the United States.

He had to go back

He grew up on a small Indiana farm and only majored in journalism in college because it seemed like the easiest course he could find. But he was blessed with an easy, natural writing style. After a short stint on a local paper, he worked his way up to reporting jobs in New York and Washington D.C., then he became managing editor of the Washington *News*. But the pressures of that life were not for him. He became a roving reporter for a chain of newspapers, and for the next few years he traveled all over the world, writing fascinating columns on a variety of subjects.

Then war broke out in Europe, and he was off to begin a phase of his career which would bring him everlasting fame. Only 5 feet 8 inches tall and weighing 110 pounds, he neither looked nor acted like a dashing war correspondent. But he wrote about the war and the American fighting men the way no one ever has. He was always where the action was, telling the story of GI Joe to millions of readers back home every day. He was there at the invasions of Italy and Sicily, and he landed in France on D-Day as Allied troops stormed ashore to begin their liberation of Nazi-held Europe. He was a friend to general and private alike, and they shared their food, their shelter, and their innermost thoughts with the soft-spoken little reporter.

By the time Paris was recaptured, he had seen enough, had watched too many friends die around him. He wrote that he was coming home. But after a few months at home, he grew restless. The war still raged on in the Pacific, and he knew he must go back. So back he went, to write of the B-29's that bombed Japan, and to land with the marines on Okinawa.

On the island of Ie Shima, as he rode in a jeep toward the front lines, a Japanese machine gun opened fire, and he was killed instantly. The entire free world mourned the passing of the reporter who had earned so much acclaim, including the coveted Pulitzer Prize for journalism. But the one tribute which would have meant the most to him was the simple monument placed on the spot where he died. It reads: "At this spot, the 77th Infantry Division lost a buddy. Ernie Pyle, 18 April, 1945."

A *revolution in food*

At only ten years of age, this New York-born youngster showed the rare combination of curiosity and ambition which would mark his fascinating career. Noticing the large number of muskrats to be found in the surrounding countryside, he asked the New York Zoo if there was a market for the animals. They gave him the name of an Englishman who was looking for muskrats, so the boy collected a dozen and sent them to England. He was paid one dollar each, the first earnings of the man who would one day become a multimillionaire.

He majored in biology in college and got a summer job as a naturalist with the Department of Agriculture. Working in New Mexico, he saw that traders were paying twenty-five cents for fur pelts brought in by trappers. He quickly checked prices with some Eastern firms, then offered the trappers twice that amount. Once again this enterprising young man realized a handsome profit, helping to pay his way through school.

The next phase of his life began after he accompanied an expedition to Labrador. Seeing the abundance of silver fox and ermine, he borrowed money and started his own fur trading company. He operated that business for the next five years, traveling thousands of miles by dogsled.

His curiosity then showed itself once more, as he made a discovery which led him into an entirely new field . . . one which would soon make his name a household word across the land.

In the icy temperatures of Labrador, which often reached sixty-five degrees below zero, he noticed something about fish which were caught through holes in the ice. They froze instantly, but when they thawed, even weeks later, the flesh was still firm and flavorful. Fascinated by this phenomenon, he began to study the possibility of quick-freezing other foods.

Returning home, he began a series of experiments, the results of which were to have tremendous effect upon the entire world. He started his first company in 1925 with the help of several investors. Some years later, he and his associates received twenty-two million dollars for their interest in the company which still bears the name of the man who pioneered the frozen food industry . . . Clarence Birdseye.

He wrote one himself

There was little in this man's background to foreshadow his eventual fame. He was the son of a prosperous landowner in New York State, and like so many sons of wealthy fathers he showed no real desire for a career of his own. He was sent to Yale, but soon got into some kind of trouble and was expelled from school. So he shipped out to sea on a merchant vessel, where he spent the next year. He found the life at sea to his liking and joined the United States Navy, spending five years in that service. After leaving the navy he returned to New York, got married, and settled down to the life of a country squire.

Always fond of books, he would often read aloud to his wife. One evening, while reading an English novel, he impatiently threw the book aside and said, "I could write you a better book than that myself." His wife merely laughed at him, so to prove his point, he actually wrote a story. It turned out so well that he decided to try a novel, but the result was less than encouraging. He had given his story an English setting, for this brand-new nation was still under the influence of British authors such as Sir Walter Scott, whose *Ivanhoe* was at the peak of its popularity.

The country gentleman-turned author was not discouraged. He decided to make a second attempt, only this time he would write an American novel, calling on his own background and experiences. His tale of the Revolution, published in 1821, became an instant success, not only in this country, but around the world as well.

Now he began to write in earnest, awakening an interest in America all over the world with his romantic tales of the early American frontier. He wrote stories about the rugged backwoodsmen who had struggled against the land to create a new nation out of a wilderness. This man, who had never written anything until he was thirty years old, produced such classics as *The Deerslayer, The Pathfinder, The Last of the Mohicans,* and many more. He was James Fenimore Cooper, America's first great novelist.

The folk tale that really was

A town in Tennessee claims him as a hometown boy. Several encyclopedias say he was born in Kentucky, while other sources claim he was actually born in Missouri, moving to Kentucky with his family as a small boy. But to many Americans the fact that he lived at all comes as a surprise, for over the years he has come to be regarded as merely a character in a folk tale, immortalized in story and song, much like Paul Bunyan or Pecos Bill.

He and his four brothers grew up in a small Kentucky town, the sons of a rural schoolteacher. At sixteen, the tall, gangly young man left school and got a job as a telegrapher with the railroad. Over the next few years he was promoted from telegrapher to brakeman, then fireman, finally realizing his ambition of becoming an engineer. He was thirty years old when the Illinois Central's crack mail train, the "Cannonball," pulled into Memphis, Tennessee, on its run from Chicago to New Orleans. The engineer was supposed to be relieved, but when he learned that his replacement was ill, he volunteered to take the rest of the run. It was nearly 4:00 a.m. when locomotive 382 struck a freight car protruding from a siding near Vaughn, Mississippi, an accident which claimed the life of only one man.

It was his friend, a black roundhouse worker named Wallace Saunders, who wrote the song which immortalized the deed of that brave engineer. He was found with one hand on the train's whistle cord and the other on the brake, having ordered his fireman to jump and save himself.

Today a museum filled with old railroad memorabilia honors his memory. On the fiftieth anniversary of the wreck, the United States Post Office issued a special stamp which bears the picture of the man who became a symbol of courage and dedication to railroad men everywhere. As the song goes, "He died at the throttle with the whistle in his hand." The date was April 30, 1900, and the engineer was the very real Casey Jones.

So painfully shy

She was born in New York in 1884. A shy and lonely child, she was afraid of many things, like dark rooms and strange people. When she was eight, her mother died of diphtheria. One year later, her father, whom she worshiped, was thrown from a horse and killed. She went to live with her grandmother, a woman who believed in Spartan discipline. There were cold baths in the morning, never any sweets, and she was taught to walk with a stick held across her back to give her better posture.

Always she suffered from that terrible shyness. Her grandmother refused to let her go to college, though the bright young girl begged to go. Instead, she was told that all she needed were a few social graces to see her through life. She became a worker at a New York settlement house, and it was there that she met her future husband. She entered into marriage still afraid, afraid of making mistakes, of not doing what was expected of her. As she later said, "For twelve years I was either having babies or getting over having one."

During World War I she joined the Red Cross, made sandwiches for servicemen, mopped floors, and helped to get a recreation center built. As her husband's career moved steadily toward fame and success, she gradually began to emerge from her shell. She became active in the cause of woman's suffrage, and more and more she was at her husband's side as he began to attain prominence.

The young girl who had been so timid and shy went on to become one of the great ladies of American history. A tireless worker for many causes, she stood courageously beside her famous husband through one crisis after another. After his death she continued her own career of public service, becoming America's first woman delegate to the United Nations, and the first head of that organization's Commission on Human Rights. When she died at the age of seventy-eight, there were three Presidents of the United States at the graveside of the woman once described as the "First Lady of the World." That was Eleanor Roosevelt.

They made him a laughingstock

This is the story of a man who had the courage to try something new for the good of mankind . . . and who spent a lifetime of frustration because of his dedication. He had discovered something, something rather ordinary which was available to practically anyone. Yet he conceived of a use for it which, for some strange reason, seemed to upset people. Despite the opposition of a conservative society, he went ahead with his experiments. One of his earliest tests was nearly a disaster because of faulty equipment. He kept on working, however, though he was now subject to more ridicule than ever.

He tried it on animals, then on himself. Satisfied

147

with the results, he gave another public demonstration, which proved successful. Yet this accomplishment was attacked by certain members of the clergy, who considered his discovery a tool of the devil, and by men of science, who accused him of fraud and quackery. He decided to try and patent his discovery, disguising its distinctive odor so that no one could infringe on his efforts. Since its very nature was so vague, he ran into hopeless legal entanglements in seeking to secure a patent. He realized now that he had been wrong in hoping to achieve material gain. What he was doing was too important to humanity. It was a discovery which belonged to the world.

Eventually, it seemed as though his lifelong dedication had borne fruit. Others began to use his discovery, and with gratifying results. The method spread to other countries, and finally the French Academy of Sciences awarded a prize for his important contribution. But even then, his triumph became clouded in controversy.

His claim to the discovery was disputed, resulting in a series of lawsuits which ruined him financially. He died, nearly penniless, at the age of forty-eight, never receiving the full credit he so richly deserved. He had been a dentist, but had spent most of his career pioneering the field of painless surgery. His name was Doctor William Morton, and he administered the first recorded surgical anesthetic. It was an invisible substance which he called letheon, but which today is known as "ether."

He captured the West

The son of a small-town newspaper publisher in New York, he had entered Yale to major in art, having shown some early ability at sketching pictures. He cared more for sports than schoolwork, and though he made the college football team, he struggled in the classroom. When his father died, leaving him a small inheritance, he left school and, shortly thereafter, fell in love with a young lady. But her father, who regarded the young man as unstable, frowned on the romance. So the adventuresome youngster decided he would head West, make his fortune, then return in triumph to claim his bride.

The husky Easterner adapted to life on the plains with surprising ease. Friendly and affable by nature, he got along well with the people of the West. He learned to handle a six-gun and a lariat, became a good rider, and worked as a cowboy on several ranches. He lived a life of freewheeling adventure for the next two years, but as his inheritance began to run out, he invested his remaining money in a Kansas ranch. It was a life which he soon discovered was not for him. Then he bought a saloon in Kansas City, and though he enjoyed that more, he made very little money.

He returned home where his girl was waiting for him, and despite her family's objections, they were married. That's when he decided to pursue, as a career, something which had only been a hobby all of his life.

He had never really abandoned his interest in art and had spent much of his spare time in sketching scenes of Western life. Now he decided to try and sell his pictures, but this, too, proved unsuccessful. With no money coming in, he went West again to prospect for gold. There he lived for a while on an Apache reservation, where he made many new drawings. He returned to New York and finally sold a picture which appeared on the cover of *Harper's Weekly*. That picture, called *Indian Scouts on Geronimo's Trail,* marked the beginning of the fabulous career of the man who captured the spirit of the frontier as no one ever had. His realistic paintings of the Indians, the rugged cowboys, and the cavalrymen he knew so well remain today as priceless mementoes of the American West. His name was Frederic Remington.

Latter-day Franklin

As a youngster he had little education, spending most of his time assisting his father in one unsuccessful business venture after another. At the age of seventeen, the young man went off on his own and took a job with a coachmaker. The aptitudes and skills which he soon displayed marked the beginning of one of the most amazingly productive business careers in American history.

He made a success out of everything he tried. After turning down his employer's offer to set him up in a business, he invented and patented a machine for cutting cloth. He built the first lawn mower, opened a furniture factory, then went into the manufacture of glue, gelatin, and isinglass. Still in his twenties, he also opened an ironworks and designed the first steam lomomotive which could draw cars around sharp curves, encouraging confidence in building railroads through difficult terrain. His locomotive, called the "Tom Thumb," was the first to be manufactured in America and was credited with saving the Baltimore and Ohio Railroad from certain bankruptcy.

He had taken a large portion of his fee in railroad stock, which increased so much in value that he became an immensely wealthy man. This enabled him to begin a number of other enterprises, including a steel rolling mill where he developed the first structural I-beam. He became president of the North American Telegraph Company and helped to lay the famed Atlantic Cable, yet the accomplishment of which he was most proud came about when he was sixty-eight years old.

Always grateful for his good fortune, he said that "the duty and pleasure of every rich man was to do something for the education and uplifting of the common people." So, in 1859, he created an educational institution which offered free instruction in engineering, art, and science. That institution, which has helped to launch the careers of many deserving Americans, still flourishes today in New York City. It is called the Cooper Union, named after the man whom one historian aptly described as a latter-day Benjamin Franklin. Peter Cooper was his name.

She made them listen

Born in South Carolina, this little black girl had to walk ten miles to school every day, past the white school, to the one-room shack which served as her classroom. She was exceptionally bright and soon learned all that she could from the local teacher. A scholarship was arranged at a school in another state, and somehow the family scraped up enough money for her train fare. It was seven years before she could get enough money for the return trip home.

She worked, put herself through college, then began teaching. Realizing the need for better schools for blacks in the South, she became determined to start a school of her own. She married and moved to Florida, and it was here that she started her school for the children of black railroad workers, beginning with an enrollment of five little girls.

Her school suffered from lack of funds, but the enterprising young teacher heard that John D. Rockefeller was staying at a nearby hotel. She marched her girls right up to the front porch where he was sitting, and before they could chase her away, she made her pitch, which was followed by a rousing spiritual by the little girls. The astounded millionaire gave her a sizable check for her efforts. After that, whenever the school needed money, she would select a likely prospect from the society pages and brazenly ask for funds to keep alive her dream of education for blacks in the South.

Now she decided it was time to try and do something for *all* of her people, and that meant going to the top. The person she wanted to talk to next was the President of the United States. She got her audience with the President, who was so moved by her appeal on behalf of her people that he made her a member of his advisory council. From that time on, her influence was felt at a national level.

When that President died, four golden chairs were set aside at his funeral for the most honored mourners . . . the President's widow, the new President, the representative of Great Britain, and the daughter of a slave, who had founded a college and had become a friend and adviser to Franklin D. Roosevelt. Her name was Mary McLeod Bethune.

Picture pioneer

Although his family had once been prosperous, and he always considered himself a Southern aristocrat, his meager
finances forced him to go to work before he completed his education. He worked for a time as a
newspaper reporter, but he felt that his real future
lay in the Broadway theater as a playwright. To
sharpen his craft he traveled as an actor, though
his heart was never really in it. But when he was
offered a job in motion pictures, he decided, with
some reluctance, to go to California, where he also
might find a market for his writing.

He soon became involved, not only in writing,

but in the actual making of films as well. With a contempt for what others were attempting to do with motion picures, he began to try some innovations of his own. He was the first to understand that stage methods didn't work in this intimate medium, so he created new cinematic techniques, like having the camera move instead of the actors. He introduced the close-up, the flashback, and the slow dissolve to end a scene. He sought out fresh, new faces for his pictures and created the star system. He made the most expensive pictures, for which exhibitors charged the highest prices, and still the public flocked to see his films and the dazzling stars he had discovered.

Despite his disdain for Hollywood, he rose to the very top of the profession. Then gradually the popularity of his pictures began to wane, as new filmakers came along. He became more bitter than ever, and within a few years he had all but dropped out of sight, a forgotten man living a lonely existence in a Hollywood hotel.

When he died the community suddenly remembered him. In typically Hollywood style they staged a spectacular funeral, as if overcompensating for the years of indifference to his contributions to the industry. Today, film festivals feature such classics as *Broken Blossoms, Intolerance,* and *The Birth of a Nation* . . . just some of the celluloid masterpieces produced by the man who first showed the world what could be done with the marvelous new medium called motion pictures. His name was D. W. Griffith.

Of letters and legends

His early life was pleasant and carefree. The youngest of eleven children, he grew up in moderately comfortable surroundings in the state of New York. Though his formal education was sketchy, he was a voracious reader encouraged by his older brothers who were members of a leading literary society. When he grew older, the personable and handsome young man studied law. Though he did become a lawyer, he never took his practice very seriously, preferring instead to spend his time tramping the beautiful Hudson River Valley near his home, communing with nature and talking with the people he met along the way.

He had always been rather frail, and his brothers, who by now were operating a prosperous hardware business, sent him to Europe for his health. After an enjoyable two years abroad, he returned to resume his law practice in New York. Then his life was marred by tragedy, when the beautiful young girl to whom he was engaged died of tuberculosis. He was sent to England to manage the branch of the family business there and quickly adapted to London society. Always a charming and witty conversationalist, he became a close friend of many of the most popular personalities of the day. He was also linked romantically with several young ladies, but the tragic death of his fiancée had left a deep scar. Though he was rumored to have had many love affairs, he remained a bachelor all of his life.

Then the family business failed, and he was suddenly faced with the necessity of earning a living. So, at the age of thirty-five, he launched the career which was soon to make him world famous.

He had done some writing earlier in his life, and now he turned to literature as a full-time career. His initial effort was the first American writing to make an impression on the rest of the world, and he went on to become one of the most important literary figures in history. Yet he is best remembered for those early stories, derived from tall tales he had heard in his youth from the Dutch settlers in his beloved Hudson River Valley. For it was he who left the world the delightful legends of such unforgettable characters as Ichabod Crane and Rip Van Winkle. He was Washington Irving.

He danced for us

The orphan boy didn't like going to school. He was raised by his grandmother, who feared that his sudden temper and his willingness to fight would be his downfall. He also had a quick wit and a ready smile, two attributes which he could rely on to keep himself out of serious trouble. He was only eight years old when he ran away to become a stable boy, the beginning of a life which would take him all over the country. It was a tough existence, and he had more than his share of fights along the way. He managed to survive, however, and in later years he had so many scars on his body that he couldn't remember where they had all come from.

The tall, rugged young man never let life get him down, never lost his irrepressible sense of humor. Fortunately, he was also the possessor of superb talent which would eventually carry him to worldwide fame. Though his career had the most humble of beginnings, he went on to become one of the most popular personalities of his time.

By the time he was sixty, he had earned and spent over a million dollars. He had a home in California, an apartment in New York, and a custom-built Duesenberg automobile. Unlike so many in his field, he never drank nor smoked. His one weakness was ice cream, which he consumed by the gallon. He never learned to read or write well, but he communicated just the same. He also invented a word which was to find its way into several dictionaries.

He appeared on the stages of the world and became a featured performer in movies as well. He was seventy-one when he died, and if asked how life had treated him, he might have answered with the word he had invented, "copacetic." Raised by a grandmother who had been a slave, he was one of the first of many black American entertainers to gain real fame and success. A dancer whose style and grace have been imitated, but never equaled, he was the original "Mr. Bojangles" . . . the fabulous Bill Robinson.

She saw the suffering

The youngest of five children, she grew up
on her father's Massachusetts farm, learning to ride almost before she could walk.
Upon completing her schooling she became a
teacher, one of the few occupations open to wom-
en in those days. After several years she moved to
Washington, D.C. and went to work in the Patent
Office, becoming one of the first women to be employed by the United States Government.

Then the Civil War began, and the capital itself
was under siege. The sight of so many wounded
young men, for whom there didn't seem to be

enough medical attention or facilities, spurred her into action. She wrote to her hometown newspaper for help, and soon the necessary food and medicine was pouring in. She became a familiar figure at the front lines, ministering to the sick and wounded with little regard for her own safety. Here, her early riding training came in handy, for often she had to leap to her horse and ride off with the enemy in plain sight.

No one can measure the lives she saved or the suffering she eased, but when the war was over she returned to Washington as a national heroine. The government honored her by creating the Department of Nursing, naming her as superintendent. Her years of working long hours without food or rest had taken their toll. She became very ill and went to Europe for a needed rest. Even there her fame had preceded her. She was visited by a group of people who had started a committee for the relief of the wounded in war. She was very impressed and made up her mind that her country would also sign their international treaty.

It wasn't as easy as she'd hoped. It took a vote of Congress for America to officially recognize the organization dedicated to the relief of those wounded in war. She never stopped campaigning, pointing out to all who would listen that such an organization would be invaluable in time of national disaster as well. It took several years, but at last she succeeded, and today that organization stands as a monument to her unselfish life. She was Clara Barton, founder of the American Red Cross.

He made a magic box

Born in a small town in the state of New York, he was, at the age of thirteen, the sole support of his widowed mother and two sisters. Leaving school in the seventh grade, he went to work as a bank messenger. By the time he was twenty-one the ambitious and enterprising young man was the bank's bookkeeper and had saved up three thousand dollars. Though he had been a loyal and hard-working employee all those years, he always had a strong sense of independence. When a relative of one of the bank's officials was promoted over him, he promptly resigned and struck out on his own in a brand-new business which was filled with financial risk.

Despite his limited formal education, he had a keen mind for things of a scientific nature. His fascination with chemistry and mechanics had kindled his interest in a hobby, something in which he foresaw a great commercial future. But the equipment in use at the time was bulky and inadequate, so he set about devising new techniques and machinery of his own. He succeeded in developing a formula which revolutionized this new industry, and he and a partner opened their own company to manufacture and distribute their goods. By the time he was thirty he was a rich man, and people all over the world were using and enjoying the products which bore his name.

A millionaire at thirty, he devoted the rest of his life to spending the money he had made. In addition to the constant development of new and better products by his company, he was one of the first to institute a profit-sharing plan so that his employees could benefit from his company's success. He founded a symphony orchestra, a music conservatory, a medical and dental school, and made enormous endowments to various universities and colleges, much of it given anonymously. In all, he gave away between seventy-five and one hundred million dollars in his lifetime. It was a fortune which began with a new method of processing film, a simple box camera, and the advertising slogan, "You press the button, we do the rest." That camera was called the "Kodak." His name was George Eastman.

Out of the saddle

He was born out West and grew up on a ranch, where he learned to ride almost before he could walk. From boyhood he was fascinated by stories of legendary horsemen and great cavalry heroes, so it came as no surprise to his friends when he persuaded his parents to let him enter a military academy. He went on to West Point and finally graduated, though his failure at mathematics had cost him an extra year there.

His first boyhood ambition was fulfilled when he was assigned to the cavalry, whose romantic, hell-bent-for-leather tradition he had so long admired. The young officer got his next lucky break when he became an aide to a general in Washington, D.C. Here was the perfect assignment, for it afforded him plenty of opportunity to ride. He became a gentleman rider, winning more than his share of steeplechase races, and he enjoyed taking part in the Sunday fox hunts as well. An excellent swordsman and pistol-shot, he was a member of the army riding team which participated in the Olympic games. After the games he took a short leave in Europe to improve his fencing technique at a famous French academy.

He got his first taste of combat when he was assigned to General Pershing's command on the Mexican border, in pursuit of the famous Pancho Villa. Encountering a trio of Villa's riders on patrol, he killed all three in a real western shoot-out. When war broke out in Europe, he again distinguished himself in action, returning home wounded.

Superb horseman, polo player, and swordsman, he was the embodiment of the cavalry officer. Yet his most famous exploits occurred when the horse cavalry had all but disappeared. Mechanization had arrived, and now they fought with tanks instead of horses. He made the transition easily, applying his lifetime of military knowledge to this new kind of warfare. During World War II, he became a legend, leading his armored divisions in lightning strikes to hasten the defeat of the Nazis in Europe. He was, indeed, the last of a long line of dashing American cavalrymen, the flamboyant, controversial officer they called "Old Blood and Guts" . . . General George S. Patton.

Gifts for America

Even in his day he was considered an eccentric, yet it never occurred to this man that there was anything unusual about his way of life. He loved people, and all the creatures and the plants of the land, regarding them as evidence of God's love. He spent his life as a wanderer, leaving his Massachusetts birthplace as a young man to discover this new country in his own way. In his first appearance in the Middle West, he was seen drifting down the Ohio River in an astonishing craft consisting of two canoes lashed together, weighted down with samples of his nature studies.

He followed a faith based upon the doctrines of Emanuel Swedenborg, a Swedish scientist, who had his own explanation of the universe. The heart of it was love: the love of God for man, and of man for God and all living things of the earth. Wherever he went, he read aloud to any who would listen from the works of Swedenborg, rolling forth denunciations in tones of thunder, followed by a cascade of jokes and merry stories gathered on his travels.

Most thought of him as a lovable, harmless lunatic. He dressed in short ragged trousers and a single upper garment of coffee-sacking with holes cut for head and arms. He was usually barefoot and wore a saucepan for a hat. But as the years went by, his cheerful nature and his kindness to people and animals made him a kind of living folk legend.

Gradually his travels took him farther and farther away from his original home. He crossed the Western plains, continuing the mission to which he had dedicated his life, and he was more than seventy years old when his journey came to an end. The world took no note of his passing, but the work he did during his lifetime will always be a part of our heritage. His name was John Chapman, and his gifts to America bear such names as "early harvest," "fall wine," "bellflower," and "russet." They can be found on the trees which remain as the living legacy of the strange and gentle man they called "Johnny Appleseed."

For safety's sake

He was born in a small village in New York State, one of ten children whose father owned a machine shop. The shop fascinated the boy, but school definitely did not. When the Civil War began, he ran away to enlist at fourteen. His father brought him back this time, but three years later he did enter the army. When the war was over he returned home to try and find a career. He enrolled in college, where he lasted only half a semester. Then he was back working in his father's machine shop for two dollars a day. Clearly, this young man had failure stamped all over him.

He had, however, a fine grasp of mechanical things, and before long he actually patented a couple of small inventions. One day he witnessed an accident involving a freight train and watched as the brakeman made a feeble and unsuccessful attempt to bring the train to a stop using the hand brake. Realizing the need for more safety in passenger trains, he set about perfecting a new kind of braking system. Like so many other things he had tried, the results of his long hours of work were not very encouraging. Then he hit upon the idea of operating railroad brakes with compressed air. He felt certain he had solved the problem, but he could find no one who would allow him to prove that his idea worked, let alone invest any money in it. Finally, after years of frustration, the Pennsylvania Railroad let him use a locomotive and a few cars for a demonstration. The results were more than he had hoped for. During the test a horse-drawn van accidentally appeared on the track, and the engineer hurriedly applied the new air brakes. The train came to a grinding halt and passengers were thrown into the aisles . . . but a man's life had been saved.

His invention of the first air brake was just the beginning for this young man. As his company grew, it expanded to many other areas of industry, including the brand-new field of electric power. For over forty years he remained active head of that company, building it into one of the true giants of American industry. His name was George Westinghouse.

A *campus radical*

One might describe this man as a revolutionary and an outside agitator. While attending school, in what was to him a foreign country, he became identified with political uprisings and disturbances. He wrote inflammatory articles while in college, spoke at protest rallies in public, and became involved in violence on behalf of the cause he believed in.

He was born on an island in the British West Indies, but because of the lack of educational facilities there, his family sent him away to school. The slender lad soon demonstrated a brilliant mind and an aptitude for learning. He intended to study law, and would probably have graduated first in his class, but the events of the day began to crowd his studies. This was a period of great political unrest throughout the land, and with typically youthful enthusiasm he threw himself into the battle.

He began to gain a reputation when he mounted an improvised platform in a public park and delivered a stirring speech. He wrote some articles and essays which were reprinted as pamphlets and caused a city-wide sensation. When the dean of the college was told they had been written by one of his students, he shook his head and said, "No boy of seventeen can write like that."

When the protest exploded into a full-scale rebellion, he was in the thick of the action, where he showed surprising military ability, good judgment, and personal courage. When the fighting ended, he was rewarded for his contributions with a high post in the new government.

The former young revolutionary went on to become a brilliant statesman, though he had an uncanny knack for making enemies along the way. Arrogant in his manner and outspoken in his views, he seemed to be constantly involved in controversy. Tragically, while still a young man, his great career was ended, but even his death had an element of drama. On July 11, 1804, the most famous duel in American history took place, as Aaron Burr shot and killed the flamboyant political figure who had been America's first Secretary of the Treasury, and one of the nation's founding fathers. He was Alexander Hamilton.

Another kind of doctor

The student's application for admittance to the medical college was greeted with consternation at the faculty meeting. No such person had ever become a doctor in the United States. The would-be student's academic background was good, but the faculty had to consider the rest of the student body. The dean feared there would be demonstrations, even violence. Yet the school could not dismiss the idea completely, for the student's application had arrived with an accompanying letter from a physician who was an extremely important figure in the profession.

The assistant professor of anatomy offered a most ingenious proposal; let the students vote on it. Surely no one could take offense at a democratic decision arrived at by fellow medical students. When the question was put to them, there was a roar of laughter at such an outlandish request, followed by a mock-serious debate. Soon satirical speeches in favor were flying about the room.

By this time, the student body was carried away with the idea of playing a glorious joke on the faculty and decided to vote in favor of admitting this minority of one to medical school.

The student was registered as No. 130, and that was how some professors chose to address this quiet revolutionary. The rest of the students watched the newcomer's reactions closely in class, for No. 130 had to work harder than anyone, with none of the social respites the rest of the students enjoyed. Even lodgings were difficult to find, until a boardinghouse owner was found who cared more about getting a year's rent in advance than what the student looked like.

When the class of 1849 graduated from Geneva Medical College, No. 130 walked last in the student procession. Yet the world's press headlined the story of that very special graduate, for she was the first woman in modern history to earn a medical degree. Her name was Dr. Elizabeth Blackwell.

A little invention

etween the years of 1832 and 1859, this man probably invented and developed a greater number of original ideas than anyone else in the world. Among his many contrivances were machinery for making nails and rivets, an ice plow, a revolver, a repeating rifle, a knife sharpener, an alarm bell for use on streetcars, a restaurant steam table, and a self-closing inkwell which was used in post offices for many years. He invented a fountain pen which was a commercial failure, but established forever the name of the instrument. He also invented a disposable paper shirt collar which, unfortunately, didn't become popular until after his death.

He had been carrying the idea for a sewing machine around in his head for several years. The machine could sew only a straight seam a few inches long, but its basic concept included a needle with an eye in its point, forming a lock stitch which would not unravel when the thread was broken . . . a true innovation which could have given him his place in history as a famed inventor. He urged his daughter to employ the new invention and go into the business of manufacturing corsets, but the year was 1838, and there was a growing belief that machinery displaced the laboring classes and was therefore immoral. Fearing that too many seamstresses would be thrown out of work, he abandoned the idea. When Elias Howe brought out a similar machine some years later, he sued, but his claim was denied because he had never applied for a patent.

It is truly ironic that the most popular of all the inventions of this little-known mechanical genius was one on which he spent less than three hours. He made it to discharge a debt of fifteen dollars he owed to a draftsman, but the man was so entranced that he insisted on paying more for all rights to the simple little device. Made out of a twisted piece of wire, it was to become nearly irreplaceable to countless millions in every walk of life and in every part of the world. The man who received the magnificent sum of four hundred dollars for that idea was named Walter Hunt, the inventor of the safety pin.

A language of our own

He was born in Connecticut in 1758 and grew up on his father's farm. He was an exceptional student and went on to college at Yale, his education interrupted briefly by his service in the army. He returned to college, graduated, and then studied law. But without enough money to open his own office, he became a teacher rather than a lawyer.

In the school where he taught, the only books available were a Bible and several spelling books from England. They were filled with names of

English kings and English places, things which meant little to these American children. So he decided to produce some books of his own, books about American people and places, filled with expressions more commonly used in the United States. He published three small books, one on spelling, one on grammar, and a reader. These books sold very well, and he thought the royalties would soon make him financially independent. But there were no Federal copyright laws in effect as yet, and others began copying and selling his books. Within a few years, however, strong copyright laws were enacted, and at last he was able to live comfortably from the earnings of his little books, which were in use in nearly every classroom in the country.

Now he could devote himself to a project he had been dreaming about: to produce a book on the English language the way it was spoken in the United States, a book emphasizing American word usage and pronunciation, not British.

His monumental undertaking took him more than twenty years to complete. He listed the origin and meaning of every word in the language, and his final manuscript contained seventy thousand entries. He later wrote that when he came to the final word, his hand trembled so much that he could hardly keep his pen on the paper. His dictionary, first published in 1828, is still the basis for most dictionaries in use today . . . a fitting tribute to the man who spent his lifetime enriching the language of America. His name was Noah Webster.

A new kind of song

 e was born in a weather-beaten shack
 in Florence, Alabama in 1873. He
 showed a remarkable ear for music at an
early age, and encouraged by his mother, he
learned the rudiments of music at a local school.
His upbringing was quite religious and his parents
strongly objected to the boy showing any interest
in the sinful music of the streets. By the time he

reached his teens he was already arranging choral parts for church groups. At the age of eighteen he left home, determined to make a living with his music. His favorite instrument was the cornet, and he joined a small band which traveled all the way to Chicago.

He worked his way back down to St. Louis, but there he found little opportunity to make a living. So he traveled from town to town, depending on his wits for food, often sleeping outside along the levee. Blacks were not welcome in most of those towns after sundown, an experience which would later play an important part in his life. Gradually his fortunes improved, and he began playing steadily with small bands and minstrel groups. He taught music at a small college for a while, then returned to the road. One night he heard some country performers move an audience with their soulful songs, a not-very-respectable type of music they called the "blues." He went right home and wrote a similar song of his own, and a whole new era in American music was born.

He called the song he wrote the *Memphis Blues*. He followed that with many more, including the *Beale Street Blues*, and, finally, the song which skyrocketed him to everlasting fame. Remembering those hungry days in hostile towns where blacks were not welcome after dark, he began the verse with the immortal line, "I hate to see that evening sun go down." The song was the *St. Louis Blues*, written by the man they called the "Father of the Blues" . . . W. C. Handy.

180

A sailor builds an empire

When he was born, the city of New York had fewer than one hundred thousand people. The boy had little formal education, but he possessed a keen mind and tremendous ambition. At the age of sixteen he borrowed a hundred dollars from his parents and bought a small boat, which had two masts and a flat bottom. He then began operating a ferry service from Staten Island to Manhattan, for which he charged the round-trip fare of twenty-five cents.

The trip was five miles long, and he often braved tricky tides and choppy waves to deliver his passengers safely. The young boatman soon earned a reputation as one of the best and hardest-working ferry pilots around, and in between passenger trips he took freight-hauling assignments to add to his income. When war broke out there was a great demand for boats to carry men and officers across the harbor to various military posts, and he began working around the clock. He soon earned enough money to buy a larger boat, and within a couple of years he owned six small schooners.

Now his eyes turned elsewhere. The steamboat had been invented, and those first boilers he saw chugging around New York Harbor fascinated him. To gain the experience he needed, he got a job as a master of a passenger steamboat, and five years later he resigned, ready now to go into business for himself. Once again he prospered, and over the next twenty years he became the king of the steamship industry, operating a huge fleet of passenger and cargo vessels along the Eastern Seaboard. When he finally sold out his shipping interests he was a millionaire, yet he had hardly begun to earn his fortune.

Again he had seen another era in transportation dawning, as the iron horse began to open up new American frontiers. He invested in railroads, and ten years later he was president of the New York Central. The ex-ferry boat pilot, who could swear like a dockhand and who was still getting into fistfights at the age of fifty, was the richest man in America when he died. Though he became this country's biggest railroad tycoon, they still called him the "Commodore." He was Cornelius Vanderbilt.

She started the fight

Though she grew up in comparative poverty, this pretty youngster managed to get an education, attending a small college where she studied nursing. She married, had three children, then returned to the nursing profession. This was hardly the background one might expect of a woman who would eventually be labeled as a purveyor of smut and corrupter of youth.

She gave up her nursing career to devote herself to another pursuit in life, one which brought her into a direct confrontation with the establishment. It started when she began publishing a newspaper

183

which attacked existing laws and agitated for reform. The language she used caused the paper to be barred from the mails and brought about her indictment on nine counts of violating obscenity laws. But her case was postponed several times, then dismissed, denying her the opportunity to bring about a head-on challenge of a law which she felt was outdated and unjust. So, in a calculated move, she and her sister opened an illegal establishment which openly dispensed unlawful material. As she expected, they were raided by the police, and she received a sentence of thirty days in jail.

After her release she continued to defy the law, and gradually some public support began to swing in her favor. Yet it was to be twenty-five years before she would begin to realize any reward from the crusade which consumed most of her adult life.

In 1873 Congress had passed a censorship regulation called the Comstock Law. Sixty-three years later, one courageous woman fought this law in the courts, finally rendering it invalid. This ruling now permitted doctors to send through the mail anything which they deemed necessary to a patient's well-being. Though the argument still rages on, the world will never forget the lifelong efforts of this dedicated woman who founded the Planned Parenthood Federation and who braved threats, insults, and jail to become the very first champion of the controversial subject of birth control. Her name was Margaret Sanger.

He loved the land

He was born and raised in central California and after high school decided to enter college to major in literature. Yet six years later he had earned only half the credits needed for a degree. He had dropped out three different times to work on ranches, in a sugar beet factory, and on a road construction crew. Still determined to be a writer, he went to New York and got a job as a newspaper reporter. He was soon fired for trying to write the news philosophically, instead of reporting the facts. He went to work as a hod carrier on a construction job, helping to build the famous Madison Square Garden. He also tried free-lance writing, but his efforts failed to set the literary world on fire.

He returned to California, where he continued to take odd jobs which would allow him enough freedom to continue writing. Finally he sold some stories, and though they brought in little money, he was encouraged enough to get married. The next few years were very rough for the couple, who lived in a cottage near the Pacific shore. Fortunately, they owned a tiny fishing boat, and for quite some time their diet consisted mainly of the fish they were able to catch. By now he was in his thirties and having serious doubts about his future as a writer.

His fortunes took a sudden upturn when a Chicago bookdealer took an interest in his work. He brought the unknown Californian's writing to the attention of a publisher, who agreed to publish a small novel which had already been rejected by nine other firms. Not only was it a success, but it was bought by Paramount Pictures and made into a movie. It was all downhill after that, as the entire world began to discover the powerful and moving style of this man who wrote with such realism of the migrant farmworkers of the Southwest, and the paisanos of his beloved Monterey Peninsula.

That first successful novel was *Tortilla Flat,* and it was followed by such classics as *Of Mice and Men* and the epic *Grapes of Wrath,* for which he won the Pulitzer Prize. These and many more fine books, including *Cannery Row* and *East of Eden,* earned him a Nobel Prize and a place among the greatest literary figures in American history. He was John Steinbeck.

He chose to be right

He was born in Virginia, the son of a Baptist minister who died when the boy was four years old. He attended school for a while, but left at the age of fourteen to go to work. He showed no great aptitude for business, but he did possess a great gift for making friends. For this tall country boy had a keen mind, a quick wit, and a great deal of natural charm.

As he grew older he continued to educate himself by reading every book he could find, and after a time he got a job as secretary to a judge, a venerable old jurist who inspired in this gawky youngster both a profound respect and a love for the law. It was only natural that he would study law himself, and after taking a special course he passed the bar examination easily.

He immediately began to make a name for himself as a criminal lawyer, where his sense of humor and easy manner enabled him to convince most juries. But after a few years he grew tired of saving clients whom he really felt should be hung. He turned to politics and was elected to the state legislature, then to Congress, where he proceeded to carve out one of the most important careers in the history of American government.

With the United States being threatened by a foreign power, he soon earned the reputation of a "hawk" for his forthright stand. He served several terms in the Senate, then in the House, and during those years his gift for oratory and his brilliant political mind made him one of the most famous and respected men in the country. No man ever wanted more to be President, yet this was the one honor which was denied him. As slavery became an issue, he enraged many of his Southern colleagues by standing firmly against secession from the Union. He summed up his defeats for the nation's highest office with the famous phrase, "I would rather be right than President." The words on a placard near his grave tell his story most eloquently. They read: "I know no North, no South, no East, no West." Those words are from a speech by one of America's truly great statesmen . . . the Honorable Henry Clay.

The athlete no one could beat

This is the story of a famous American whose father raised seven children on a factory worker's meager pay. With no extra money for idle entertainment, he built sports equipment for the kids to use, filling the backyard with exercise bars, trapezes, and weights. It's no wonder that the children of this family were the best athletes in town.

One of the kids became a basketball star in high school and later the top player for a local team sponsored by an insurance company. When the company decided to sponsor a track and field team, the basketball star became its best track performer as well.

There were many large teams of athletes on hand for the Olympic trials held that year in Evanston, Illinois. But one team had only a single entrant, a super athlete who entered four events and won more points individually than any other team in the field. Then came the Olympic games, and this same track sensation won two gold medals, setting a world's record in one event. The sports pages were filled with the exploits of this new phenomenon, who one day decided to give up track and field to concentrate on a brand-new sport, where a whole new world of fame and fortune lay ahead.

The new game was golf, and it didn't take long for an athlete with this kind of talent and coordination to master it. One tournament after another was captured by this long-hitting pro, soon acknowledged as the best in the game. Then, at the peak of a brilliant career, tragedy struck. The diagnosis was cancer, the only thing which was ever to defeat this gallant champion.

No one grieved more than the person closest to this all-time superstar . . . her loving husband. Yes, this great champion was a woman, probably the finest woman athlete who ever lived. Basketball star, Olympic recordholder, and a golfer so good that she was barred from entering men's tournaments, she was Mildred Didrikson Zaharias. We all called her "Babe."

To help a great lady

He was born in Budapest, Hungary, and this frail son of a Hungarian-Jewish father and an Austrian mother came to this country penniless at the age of seventeen. After service in the Union army during the Civil War, he settled in St. Louis, where he continued his education. He earned a law degree, and before long he was involved in politics and business as well.

At the age of thirty-one he entered the field in which he was to spend the rest of his life, when he purchased two almost defunct newspapers. He merged them and soon was the publisher of a successful and profitable paper. Within a few years he used his profits to buy a paper in New York, eventually building a publishing empire of great power and influence across the nation.

The former immigrant became an important and wealthy man. He never forgot his humble beginnings, however, and displayed a fierce love for his adopted country, whose ideals of freedom and justice had given him the opportunity to make good. Few people know the role he played in making one of America's greatest landmarks a reality.

The Statue of Liberty had been given to the United States as a gift from the people of France, to stand at the entrance of New York Harbor as a welcome to refugees from all over the world. When the statue was finished, it was discovered that it would take one hundred thousand dollars to erect a pedestal upon which the "Great Lady" would stand. The American government was asked to appropriate the money and refused. It looked as though the statue would never reach its destination.

The generous gift from the people of France might have remained crated and forgotten in Europe, had it not been for the efforts of one man. Through his newspapers he began a campaign to raise the needed funds, and within a few months the American people had contributed enough pennies, nickels, and dimes to erect a base for the mighty statue which has become a symbol of freedom. That was the proudest accomplishment of the immigrant who also bequeathed millions to the encouragement of literature in America. The publisher of the St. Louis *Post-Dispatch*, the New York *World*, and the founder of our most coveted literary award, his name was Joseph Pulitzer.

He remembered the plans

He was born in humble surroundings on a Maryland farm, where the only tools available were crude rakes and plows. Yet as a tiny boy he first displayed his incredible mechanical aptitude by fixing those simple implements to make them work better. In school he showed an amazing facility with mathematics, and an interest in science as well. He also became somewhat of a naturalist, learning everything he could about the plant and animal life around him.

Though his formal schooling ended at fifteen, he continued his education by reading and observing. He once borrowed a watch from his mother, took it apart to see how it worked, then put it back together in perfect working order. A short time later he followed those principles in building a wooden clock, one which kept exact time and also struck the hour. It was probably the first clock ever completely built in America. He became interested in astronomy and became so knowledgeable on the subject that he was able to predict an eclipse.

His brilliance came to the attention of the Secretary of State, Thomas Jefferson, and he was appointed to the surveying team which was laying out the District of Columbia as our nation's capital. When the project's chief architect was dismissed, he angrily took all his plans with him. But the man whom Jefferson had singled out justified his appointment by amazingly reproducing those plans from memory.

This scientific and mathematical wizard published a popular almanac filled with his accurate predictions about the weather and the tides, plus other invaluable information. When he had completed his first almanac he sent a copy to Thomas Jefferson, who was so impressed that he sent it on to the French Academy of Arts and Sciences in Paris, with the result that this American was made a member of that respected body. But equally as important was the letter which accompanied the almanac, a letter which made Jefferson and many others reflect upon the intellectual potential of the Negro for the very first time. For this eminent scholar, one of America's first important men of science, was a black man, the son of a slave. His name was Benjamin Banneker.

A sailor at heart

His father was prominent in the business and social life of the young city of New York, and his mother was descended from a long line of shipowners and merchant seamen. By the time he was seven, the boy had one passionate desire . . . to be a sailor. He built boats, gathered specimens for a marine museum, and spent the happiest times of his life at the family's summer home on the Atlantic Seaboard.

His longing to follow the sea became stronger with the years, and he proved his aptitude for the calling by the ease with which he learned to navigate a sailboat. But when it came time to decide the boy's future, his father put his foot down. The lad was sent to a leading prep school to prepare for an academic career, instead of fulfilling his dream of attending Annapolis.

Angry at his father's decision, he worked out a plan with a school friend to run away and enlist in the navy. They had arranged with a pie man to have themselves smuggled out of school in his delivery wagon, but when the great day came, the pie wagon left the school without its secret cargo. The two renegades had come down with the measles and were quarantined in the school infirmary.

He went on to college, eventually putting aside his thoughts of a naval career for another kind of public service. He entered politics, where he soon displayed a rare quality of understanding the needs of the common man. His rise was rapid, and despite personal tragedy, he overcame great obstacles to become one of the most important figures in modern American history. Yet in a curious way he was also able to attain his ambition of holding a post in the United States Navy.

At one point in his political career he actually served as Assistant Secretary of the Navy, though he relinquished that post to become governor of his state. Then, some fourteen years before his death, he finally received his commission, holding a rank which far exceeded his boyhood ambition. For he became Commander in Chief of all the military services in his role as thirty-second President of the United States. He was Franklin Delano Roosevelt.

This bright and gifted girl lived in the state of Maine until her teens, then moved with her family to Santa Barbara, California. She completed her schooling, then entered the field of elementary education. She operated a private kindergarten for a time, then went to San Francisco where she established the first free kindergarten west of the Rockies. When she married, she gave up her school and moved East.

After her husband died, she remarried and began a writing career, turning out a succession of popular children's books which seemed to reflect

197

the warmth, charm, and intelligence of the lady who wrote them. She was later to write her autobiography, in which she told of an incident which occurred when she was a little girl, a chance meeting which was to have a profound effect upon her life.

At twelve the little girl was already a voracious reader, and one author in particular was her favorite. As fate would have it, she and her mother took a train to visit relatives in another city, and on that train she caught sight of the famous writer himself, who was visiting America on a lecture tour. While her mother was occupied, the child slipped away to the next car where she found the great man sitting alone. She promptly sat down beside him and introduced herself, and for the next hour the two engaged in an animated conversation. He was astounded at her knowledge of his books, and she confessed that she had read one of them six times. He, in turn, was charming, gracious, and totally delighted by this bright, smiling child. Though they never saw each other again, she would always remember every detail of that day.

Her lovely children's stories made her a famous author in her own right, and one of them became one of the best-selling books of the twentieth century. She always knew that the spark which made her become a writer was kindled on that day in 1868, when a little girl found a friend on a train . . . Charles Dickens. Her name was Kate Douglas Wiggin, author of the classic and beautiful story titled *Rebecca of Sunnybook Farm*.

Small but mighty

is first job was as a bobbin boy in a cotton mill. He was thirteen years old and worked twelve hours a day for the sum of $1.20 a week. That was fine with him, because he knew he was destined for bigger and better things. His father had been a weaver in Scotland, and he had borrowed money to bring his family to America, where he knew there was plenty of opportunity for those who were willing to work hard.

His son believed it, too, and when the little Scot, who was to remain small in stature all his life, got a job at the telegraph company for the magnificent sum of $2.50 a week, he exclaimed, "Anyone could get along in this country." No more prophetic words were ever spoken. His new job brought him to the attention of many influential people, among them the superintendent of the Pennsylvania Railroad. He became a telegraph operator for the railroad, where he impressed everyone with his intelligence and his willingness to accept responsibility. In a couple of years he was promoted to manager of the railroad's western division.

About that time he made his first investment, buying a few shares of stock. Then he became interested in a new invention, the first railroad sleeping car. He induced the Pennsylvania Railroad to build and operate a few of these cars, and for his efforts he was rewarded with an interest in the brand-new company. That interest soon became the cornerstone of his financial future. By the time he was thirty-three, he had made over fifty thousand dollars in a single year, but that was only the beginning.

He continued to invest, adding his intelligence and his energy to such ventures as a bridge company, iron mills, and finally, steel. Combining sharp business sense with a sometimes reckless imagination, he operated on a simple theory: "Have faith in America," he said, "every financial flurry is the prelude to prosperity greater than ever before." Those were the words of the little Scotsman who started at a salary of $1.20 a week and went on to become the wealthiest man in America and one of the most important philanthropists in our history. His name was Andrew Carnegie.

BIBLIOGRAPHY

Armbruster, Maxim E. *The Presidents of the United States, and Their Administrations from Washington to Nixon.* 5th ed. rev. New York: Horizon Press, 1973.

Benet, Laura. *Famous American Poets.* New York: Dodd, Mead & Co., 1950.

Bolton, Sarah K. *Famous American Authors.* Revised by William A. Fahey. New York: Thomas Y. Crowell Co., 1954.

_____. *Lives of Poor Boys Who Became Famous.* rev. ed. Edited by Margaret Wilson. New York: Thomas Y. Crowell Co., 1962.

Cooke, Donald E. *Atlas of the Presidents.* Maplewood, N. J.: Hammond, 1967.

Cooper, Alice C., and Palmer, Charles A., eds. *Twenty Modern Americans.* New York: Harcourt, Brace & Co., 1942.

Faber, Doris, and Faber, Harold. *American Heroes of the Twentieth Century.* New York: Random House, 1967.

Garraty, John A., and Sternstein, Jerome L. eds. *Encyclopedia of American Biography.* New York: Harper & Row, 1974.

Great Lives, Great Deeds. Pleasantville, N.Y.: Reader's Digest Association, 1964.

Hurwitz, Harold L. *Encyclopedic Dictionary of American History.* New York: Washington Square Press, 1970.

Hylander, Clarence J. *American Inventors.* New York: Macmillan Co., 1964.

Kronenberger, Louis, ed. *Atlantic Brief Lives: A Biographical Companion to the Arts.* Boston and Toronto: Little, Brown & Co., An Atlantic Monthly Press Book, 1971.

Lavine, Sigmund. *Famous Industrialists.* New York: Dodd, Mead & Co., 1961.

_____. *Famous Merchants.* New York: Dodd, Mead & Co., 1965.

Mersand, Joseph, ed. *Great American Short Biographies.* New York: Dell Publishing Co., 1966.

Mini-Sketches of Great Americans. St. Louis Board of Education. New York: Washington Square Press, 1974.

Morgan, James. *Our Presidents: Brief Biographies of Our Chief Magistrates from Washington to Eisenhower, 1789-1958.* 2d enl. ed. New York: Macmillan Co., 1958.

Prindiville, Kathleen. *First Ladies.* New York: Macmillan Co., 1964.

Reinfield, Fred. *The Great Dissenters: Guardians of Their Country's Laws and Liberties.* New York: Thomas Y. Crowell, 1959.

Sobol, Donald J. *Lock, Stock and Barrel.* Philadelphia: The Westminster Press, 1965.

Stevens, William O. *Famous Scientists.* New York: Dodd, Mead & Co., 1952.

Stoddard, Hope. *Famous American Women.* New York: Thomas Y. Crowell Co., 1970.

Webster's American Biographies. Edited by Charles Van Doren. Springfield, Mass.: G. & C. Merriam Co., 1974.

World Book Encyclopedia. 22 vols. Chicago: Field Enterprises, 1974.

Author's Note: For further reading on historical people, places, and events, *American Heritage* is highly recommended. *American Heritage* is published every two months by American Heritage Publishing Co., New York.

ALPHABETICAL LISTING

ALPHABETICAL LISTING